Writing from the Inner Self

Writing from the Inner Self

ELAINE FARRIS HUGHES

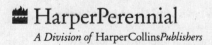
HarperPerennial
A Division of HarperCollinsPublishers

Grateful acknowledgement is made for permission to reprint:

Lines from Stephen Sondheim's "Finishing the Hat" from *Sunday in the Park with George*, © 1984. Reprinted by permission of Revelation Music Publishing Corp. & Rilting Music, Inc., A Tommy Valando Publication.

Shinkichi Takashi's poem "Potato" published in *Leaping Poetry*, edited by Robert Bly, Boston: Beacon Press, 1972. Reprinted by permission of the translator, Harold P. Wright.

Designed by Helene Berinsky

The Library of Congress has catalogued the hardcover edition as follows:

Hughes, Elaine.
    Writing from the inner self / Elaine Farris Hughes.
      p.   cm.
    Includes bibliographical references and index.
    ISBN 0-06-016572-3 (cloth)
    1. English language—Rhetoric—Problems, exercises, etc. I. Title.
PE1413.H84 1991   90-4630
808'.042—dc20

ISBN 0-06-272023-6 (pbk.)
     95 96 RRD 10 9 8 7

For Stefanie Woodbridge,
who returned me to the pleasures of writing
and
For my students
Who inspired this book

Contents

The wine still waits in the cellars below.

My beloved family still sits on the porch in the dark.

The fire balloon still drifts and burns in the night sky of an as yet unburied summer.

Why and how?

Because I say it is so.

—RAY BRADBURY
Preface, Dandelion Wine

Prologue:
Bean Picking

You go out to the garden with a basket on your arm. Three people want beans for dinner. At first the pickings are so slim that you think you'll have to run out and buy beans or maybe just have carrots instead.

With each bean you pick, you think that this is the last one—there don't seem to be any others. Yet you keep finding another bean and then another. You're so busy looking and picking that you don't even notice the bottom of the basket, which is already covered with the long green pods.

When no more beans are in sight, you get down on your knees and search under the bushes. At first your eyes can't pick out the green beans nestled into the green leaves. But you stay with it. Soon your eyes grow accustomed to what they are looking for and you begin to find hidden treasures—many beans in clusters, others resting on the ground waiting for you.

Even so, moments come when you feel impatient with these tiny creatures playing hide-and-seek with you. Moments come when you feel that you're not going fast enough. There are many other things back in the house that need your attention. Picking these beans is interfering with your life.

But the beans don't understand that. They want to wait where they have ripened for your table until you can find them. They've done their job. Now they want you to do yours. So you keep picking. Some of them are not ripe yet. Others have decayed and have to be discarded. Some are so tiny that you think you should throw them away. But you need beans, so you toss them into your basket.

Finally, you've done all you can. You rise, look up at the sky, listen to the birds, take in the canvas of leaves above you, and breathe deeply. The hard part is over. You see that the basket overflows. Each little bean that you harvested has helped to fill it, and now there will be beans for three tonight at dinner. You make your way back to the kitchen, humming a little tune. Something in you remembers that this is how it always is. Yes, bean by bean—that's how everything gets done.

Part I

PRELIMINARIES

——— On Writing ———

Nobody else can write what you can write. You are one of a kind and have had one-of-a-kind experiences. And, on top of that, nobody else sees or feels exactly what you see and feel. Right this very minute, you've got enough material stored within you to write a shelffull of books.

I don't mean to make writing sound as simple as playing the radio—I have too much respect for the demands writing makes on a person to do that. But I'm convinced that most people are born story tellers and that the act of writing can be a pleasure. It can be your recreation, your inspiration, your job, your friend, your teacher. To sum it up, I believe in writing. I think the act of writing can change lives and save souls. I've seen it happen.

And who doesn't want to write? I've rarely met anyone who didn't eventually confess a secret yen to write something important "someday." The motivations vary—some think it'll get them on Phil Donahue, some think it'll make them rich, some fantasize about the free-wheeling life of a writer. But there is some magic pull for nearly everyone about writing.

Yet the act of writing looms higher than Mount Fuji for many of us. Rather than the integrative activity it could be, it becomes yet another outside event which pulls us away from ourselves. We have to write papers, memos, letters, reports. We have to meet deadlines. We have to convince, entertain, impress others. Soon we discover that there is *nobody at home* in our writing. Certainly, we ourselves are not there. Some sputtering machine has taken up residence and is spewing out dead words that mean nothing to anyone—especially to us. We have forgotten that any writing worth reading has to originate from some genuine place within us.

My own relationship with writing changed for the good once I realized that all my writing is mostly for me—and comes only from me. I decide that I'll write, I choose the project, or it chooses me, and then I become the instrument by which it gets written. I have even come to understand that I don't have to like everything I write. My job is just to be the scribe, to write one piece and then go on to the next.

I've found that the major starter for me in anything I write is *voice.* I can't take a step until I get the voice that's going to write that particular piece. What I mean by voice is that as I'm writing some real person seems to be there. I actually hear a voice as I write. When that doesn't happen, I'm stuck; when it does happen, then I can feel my muscles and bones flexing and warming up to write. Most of the time that voice is one of my own: the scared me, the schoolteacher me, the irreverent me, the raunchy me or whatever. I recognize each of them as one of the voices I walk around with in my head. The most exciting moments, however, come when the voice is that of a visitor, a person I don't know, who comes and takes over my awareness and my writing for a while. When these people drop in and tell me about themselves, I find myself writing things I never even thought of before.

The exercises in this book are designed to help you discover as many of your own voices as possible and to open you to other voices as well. I hope the exercises will lay the groundwork for that moment when "something" takes over and you find yourself writing for hours—totally absorbed and having fun. Start your writing from the inside, from a place within where the real you lives. Begin with yourself—dip into your memories, feelings, body sensations, observations, imagination, and make something exist that was not there before.

I'll walk along with you for a while, encouraging you to find that point of ease in your writing that feels like your true and natural self. I hope you'll soon come to feel that you're not a writer struggling with words, but a human being through whom writing can flow into existence.

—— *Keeping a Journal* ——

Anytime I feel old, finished, used up, or find myself asking "What's the point of living anyway?" I pull my old journals off the shelf and sit down to read. Seeing myself through the tunnel of memory puts the past in its place and helps me to see that life keeps on coming—and that it is doing that right now. The woman in those journals struggling to make sense of her existence seems to be making tracks, seems once again to be worthy of my attention and empathy. I come away from the reading of these old journals energized, ready to live again, and even boiling up with something to write about.

But I don't only gain perspective from keeping a journal; I also stay a bit saner. When the forces mash down on me, I pick up my journal and write rather than taking violent action against myself or others. And sometimes when I forget that I've ever written a decent word, I stumble onto a shining tidbit and think happily, *Did I write that? That's pretty good* So I can't sing enough praises about journal-keeping.

If you already keep a journal, then I don't have to convince you. Most people, once they discover the riches of keeping a journal, are hooked forever and tote their journals everywhere they go. But in case you need a little convincing, I'll give you my schoolteacher lecture on journal-keeping.

Keeping a journal can turn you into a writer faster than anything else I can think of. It keeps you in contact with yourself and helps you put your thoughts and feelings into words on the spot—so you use writing as a way to discover what you think and feel.

Immediately you have writing with substance. You have a genuine voice and something to say. Journals also help you develop your own personal writing styles—they give you a chance to experiment in miniature. You'll often find that some of your journal entries can be developed into complete essays or stories. Because you are writing for yourself and not some amorphous audience, you'll find yourself freer, more confident, and sometimes more outrageous than when you're doing "real" writing. And a journal can knock a hole through almost any writer's block if you treat it as attentively and with as much appreciation as you do a good friend. It stands ready to serve as your audience, your therapist, your lover, and your archivist.

Make your journal a record of your inward journey, not just a day-by-day description of what you do. Don't treat your journal the way you did those old diaries you might have kept in grade school, in which you recorded every detail of the big weekend and every fight with your best friend. A journal should be something like an inner landscape—a picture of how and where you are at a given time. Many famous writers have kept journals faithfully and have published excerpts from them. If you need further inspiration for starting your own, look at the journals of Anaïs Nin, Virginia Woolf, André Gide, Lawrence Durrell, Annie Dillard, May Sarton, Thomas Merton, or Stephen Spender, to name a few.

A final word: Don't worry about correctness. Write as spontaneously and as honestly as you can and let your thoughts and words flow freely. Don't stop to censor your thoughts or find the "right" word or check your spelling and all that. After you've written, you can go back, proofread, and make any corrections and adjustments you want so that you're satisfied you've said just what you mean. Remember, this journal is for *you*. And it will reward you in countless ways.

SUGGESTIONS FOR JOURNAL ENTRIES

As a way to vary your journal entries and try out different modes of writing you might use some of the following suggestions. Don't forget to date your entries—one day you'll be glad you did.

Survey your accomplishments over the past six months.

Write down what you think about men (or women).

Put on a piece of instrumental music and let it lead and shape your writing.

Catalog every little thing that is right about you.

Respond to today's news.

Set down a bright idea you've carried around in your head for awhile.

Philosophize—about life in general or people in particular.

Write about the biggest challenge you now face.

Describe your favorite room.

Respond to a book, a movie, a record.

Take ten minutes to write out a solution to a current problem.

Record some unusual data you've collected.

Create a game plan for completing a current project.

Copy a favorite poem or passage of writing and interpret it.

Turn a page into a scrapbook to hold a picture, ticket stubs, a flower and write about its significance for you.

Analyze your most negative characteristic; praise your most positive one.

Speculate on where you'll be next year and what you'll be doing.

Fantasize about the big trip you're going to take one day.

Write what you think and feel about writing.

Recall an object that used to be important but has now disappeared.

Remember your most hated childhood foods.

Recollect an article of clothing you once loved.

List all your favorite songs or books from a particular year.

Do an inventory of the new things you've learned this year.

Compile a list of all your favorite short quotations.

Sit in front of a painting and write your thoughts and impressions.

Try your hand at writing a poem or song.

Speculate on the historical importance of today's date.

Describe your most romantic moment.

Tell a story about your long-ago neighbors.

Shoot the moon: Write about what it means to you to be *alive*.

— *Facing the Brick Wall* —

You put down a few scraggly words . . . and then another few.
You take a breath and wait. Other words come. You proceed on
faith that more words will continue to come in some form or
other. At last you're writing again.

Yes, writing is always an act of faith. It takes courage and a
belief in all that's not readily seen to continue to write. But if you
haven't yet developed this long-abiding faith, you can't always
know that millions of words belong only to you and will come to
you day in and day out, that all you really have to do is be there,
open your arms, and catch a bundle.

So why do many of us become wordless when we stare at a
blank piece of paper? Well, we'll deal with that next; but before
I go a step further, let me give you some advice: Do *not* be
intimidated by those who write regularly, constantly, effortlessly.
There are lots more of us than there are of them. Most of the
people I know who write struggle with a resistance to writing—
better known as writer's block.

I've often wondered about writer's block. What is it actually?
How does it feel? Is it even real? I often see it as a big brick wall
staring me down; I often feel it as a cement block somebody has
dropped on my head. When it comes to visit, it can stay for thirty
minutes or thirty days. When I get writer's block, I make myself
so busy that I couldn't write even if I wanted to, and then I walk
around wringing my hands and sighing, "I just want to write
. . . I'd give anything to get back to writing." Sometimes I can
carry on this little drama for months.

This next paragraph should logically explain how I have over-come writer's block, but that's not what's going to happen. In-stead I'm going to tell you more about my writer's block. My blocks about writing seldom have anything to do with words being unavailable to me. I can open my mouth to say three words and out tumble three hundred and fifty. So getting words together is not my problem. My particular blocks show up as dogged resistance to doing what I said I'd do. This can range from refusing to do the morning writing stint I promised myself to failing to complete a project that's due any minute.

What I've been learning about this is that a block is actually nothing more than a *resistance.* And this resistance is often a clue that my direction, my commitment, my viscera have not yet been hooked. I haven't quite discovered the kernel that contains the flowering seed.

So what do I do? In the past I'd whip myself like an old donkey and try to get my feet plodding again. And that's all they did—plod. Now I do that new number called free-writing. I write nonstop without going back to read. I write *through* the resist-ance. I simply plow ahead and get hundreds of useless words down on paper until a single sentence or two or three pop right out at me and announce themselves as "the truth." Then I can coax myself into continuing by beginning with one or two ideas or sentences that mean something to me. I ask myself very sweetly: "Where do you want to go next?" I've found that nearly always the good stuff is going to be behind the resistance. Often my best pieces of writing come hand-in-hand with my strongest resistance.

You can see where this is leading. *The only cure for writer's block is to write.* It's probably disgusting to hear that miserable idea again. But there's no help for it because it's true. It's true what all those writers' magazines have been telling us for years. *Write.* That's all there is to it. Write about your writing block, write about the pigeon on your apartment ledge, write about your latest success (or failure) in love, write about why you hate what you're writing, write about your great-aunt in Omaha who wears army boots, write about the planter's wart that drives you crazy.

Now here's a tip for your inner critic, that strict purse-lipped nonperson who stands around commenting sourly on everything you write. Be friendly. Smile. Tickle it in the ribs. Learn to coexist. In my writing group, we have a ritual; we each hold up our pieces of writing before we start to read and announce, "This is a piece of shit." Everybody nods in agreement, says, "Yeah, yeah, now get on with it." And then we carry on and read anyhow, and the critic takes a short nap. Truth is, much of writing is just standing up to that devil critic and daring the fires of hell to touch you. In spite of what your critic says, you are entitled to write.

And, since you can always sidle around the brick wall and through the back door, here are some tips to help you when you're stuck and find even the exercises in this book too much to handle. Use the tips, lists, and story starters however and whenever you like. All I ask is that you be very kind to yourself about your writer's block—*starting right now.*

TEN WRITING TIPS FOR WRITER'S BLOCK

Write about what you would write about if only you didn't feel blocked.

Write about what you will—at some future point—actually write about. (You can start with a list and expand it with descriptions at a later date.)

Write about your ideal game plan for completing a writing project. (Maybe, "I'll feel over the hump when I have. . . ." Follow with a list.)

Write the smallest possible segment of a larger piece. Instead of a whole story or even a paragraph, concentrate on an opening sentence or a 100-word description of someone's hat. Working in miniature can often warm your creative juices to more writing.

Write a list of subjects you *want* to write about one of these days.

Write down what you think you can accomplish on your writing goal or project *for today only.* Don't think beyond today, and force yourself to put down less than you think you can do.

Write down what you overhear other people say. Steal lines while you're in a café or on a bus. You'll be amazed at how lyrical some of it is. You can arrange all the lines into a poem or write some dialogue. At any rate, this tip will at least get you out of the house.

Write for 7 (*only* 7) minutes. Set a timer or an alarm and, when it rings, force yourself to stop. If you're miserable in your writing, then you're saved. If you're ecstatic in your writing, so much the better. By having to quit you'll be panting to get back soon.

Write in detail about every single thing you did yesterday. (Did you do any writing of any kind? Give yourself credit if you did.)

Write a log of every minute you spend each day on *any* writing. Start now. This is especially important if you are working toward a specific goal. Keeping a log might hurt at first, but think of it as giving yourself credit for every moment you spend writing when you could easily be doing something else.

A LIST OF LISTS

Some days when you are absolutely stuck—I mean so stuck that you can't even get six words together in your head—you can try another way out.

Just choose a topic from the following list and make a random and very rapid list. Keep at it even though you feel you've exhausted your brain. Set the clock for about 10 to 15 minutes and don't stop until time's up. You might find yourself sparked into actual writing by some of the words that tumble out uncensored.

Sensuous Pleasures

Future Daydreams

Things I'm Keeping from Myself

Good Things about My Writing

Ways I'm Unkind to Myself

Unusual Experiences I Have Had

The Masks I Wear

Sexual Wants (or Don't Wants) Right Now

All the Things That Are O.K. about Me

Old Yearnings

New Ambitions

All the Things I Want That Money *Can* (or Can't) Buy

Physical Ailments That Plague Me

Pieces I Want Someday to Write

People I Miss

Childhood Delights

Things That Do Not (or Do) Work in My Life

Some Gratitudes

Why I'll Never Be (or *Will* Be) a Writer

Favorite Books (Songs, Plays, Movies)

Future Fantasies

Secrets

Feelings That Cause Me the Most Trouble

Memorable Moments

Objects I Have Loved

STORY STARTERS

Occasionally it helps to be told what to write. If you're stuck for a writing idea, try using one of the following sentences for an opening to get you started. It's also fun to work the other way and write a short piece that ends with one of the sentences. (Pay attention to which ones your mind immediately fills in.) Use as many words as you like for each blank.

Just as the _____, they decided to _____.

In a wild hour of _____, Matthew _____ that would _____ forever.

Sometimes things happen to you before you're ready for them. Take, for instance, _____.

I opened the door and there he (she) stood. I said _____.

While she was watching the _____, Letitia got the idea for _____.

Harvey never even imagined himself in such a situation. Now he _____.

When the _____ fell, they were _____.

Looking at the situation, Melanie was tempted to _____ before the _____.

The girl, confused and angry, looked _____ where the _____ and _____.

He walked over the _____ and _____. "They're not here yet," he hollered. He seemed anxious.

Some things never change. Last night, I _____.

Mrs. Harding looked at _____ with concern. Then she _____.

"You'll need a _____," said the man behind the counter.

As a rule, Lucinda never spoke to strangers. But _____.

If you _____, you are likely to _____.

You can also try these titles for some whimsical writing:

Alphon Gertrose and the Amazing Bubble Machine
Superwoman and the Rain of Popcorn

The Four Blood Sisters and the World Bazaar
Roland and Rita and the Zodiac Cruiser
The Blind Pickpocket and the Missing Girdle

ON NOT BEING ABLE TO FINISH

I wonder if other writers have as much trouble finishing a piece as I do. I have trouble finishing—*putting an end to*—almost anything I write. I suspect that there are countless writers like me who have boxes of unfinished manuscripts which they've hidden from themselves for fear of finishing them. Perhaps you're one of them.

It's not always "finding an ending" that's a problem. I finally have figured that out. Often I know exactly how I want a piece to end, but then I put it away before I write the ending and sometimes succeed in hiding it from myself for months. I don't want to let go of it or have it let go of me, because it will be over. Done with. Dead words on paper. No more life. Then I'll start another piece, because each new piece has stretched out before it only the possibility of getting finished and that sustains me for a while. But when that one nears the rim of completion, I put it away too, because every ending feels like a loss to me and I already feel as if I've lived through enough losses. I can't control most losses—the deaths of those I love, the end of relationships, the carnivorous clock—but I can certainly control the ending of a piece of writing and save myself one more loss.

For instance, I wrote the first three drafts of this book on the crest of creation—having fun, feeling buoyed up by my ideas, admiring myself for meeting the challenge with discipline and fortitude. Then time came to *finish* the final manuscript. Serious business. I got sick, couldn't sleep at night, couldn't bear to look at it. I thought for a while that I had escaped the old headless horseman on this trip, but that turned out to be an illusion. I found myself right back in the ditch, crying for a rescue team. I knew then that I would either have to take a sledgehammer to the manuscript and dismantle it so I could start all over, or I would have to let it go, give it up, finish it before it finished me. I tricked myself into giving it up by taking time out to start another book. Once I got a dozen pages done on the new one, I felt safe enough to let this one go.

I now understand and accept that ending any piece of writing is, for me, exactly like a death—the death of one of my most intimate companions with whom I've been living intensely. And perhaps equally important, it is the death of yet another dream of perfection. To end a piece which you know is not yet perfect is to doom it to a flawed existence forever. It takes guts to give it your blessings and let it go find its own destiny.

On Meditation

There are voices in you that want to be heard. The voices are tiny, low, delicate. As you walk around talking to others, balancing your checkbook, making phone calls, buying groceries, the little voices constantly murmur way down inside of you. There are memories and stories in you that want to be told. Under each of them lie layers of possibility. Each little fragment is tightly bunched with incredible meaning, strands upon strands that can lead you in many different directions. But to get to these stories, these voices, and form them into your creation, you first have to meet them down inside yourself. You have to travel down to get them. And meditation is one of the easiest ways to travel there.

It's all pretty scientific. In fact, it was scientists who discovered that our brain functions on several levels: Beta, Alpha, Theta, and Delta, with Beta being the highest frequency of brain waves and Delta the lowest. Most of our conscious living is done in the Beta state where we live in an outer world bursting with honking horns, television sets, incessant talking, and circular thinking. This is our normal waking state where we get the business of daily life done, but often at great cost to ourselves. What saves us is that we sleep and dream, spend regular time in the Theta and Delta states so that we repair ourselves enough to face life in the Beta lane again.

But we're more interested here in the Alpha state, the level most often under used or ignored. The Alpha state is the *meditative* state, that level of mind somewhere between waking and sleeping, we are awake, aware of our surroundings, but more tuned into our inner consciousness rather than the outside world.

In this state of mind, we become relaxed and refuel our energies. We solve problems easily, touch base with our intuitions, romp around in creative play. All of us recognize this state, because suddenly everything seems just fine—we are breathing deeply and feeling in harmony with ourselves and the world. Bright ideas seem to pop out of nowhere into our heads.

So this is how it all fits in with writing: The Alpha state gives us a fertile place to write from and more to write about. The Beta state, the place we know best, is filled with less complex thinking and information, the stuff most likely to pop out first. Behind this front-rank line of conscious, predictable information, however, lies the deep and timeless reservoir of our inner consciousness, a vast source of unique material. This level, available to us in the Alpha state, contains our most important memories, as well as our most original ideas and impulses. From this source we can discover limitless possibilities for self-expression, in this case writing. Getting to this source doesn't take so much time and effort— mostly a willingness to travel. By taking the time to travel inward to connect with a feeling, an idea, an image, a memory, a body sensation—some almost tangible substance—you will find yourself with something important, even urgent, to say.

The meditation techniques in the following chapter and the exercises in Part II can give you practice in combining these inward journeys with your writing, and the more you practice, the more easily you will get there. You don't have to be a student of meditation to use these techniques, either; just following the simple directions will get you to another place deep within.

These meditation techniques, while they can't be considered "real" meditation—that long process leading to a relaxed state of emptiness—are still sufficient to take you to a level of greater creativity. Think of them as mini-forays into your inner consciousness, a place where you can go to dip into your own reservoir of remarkable material whenever you like.

— *Meditation Techniques* —

I've been using little meditations in my teaching for many years. I stumbled upon the idea while trying to get my students to "see" something before they wrote so that their writing would be concrete and vivid. All of the meditation techniques I use in the classroom are necessarily brief because the emphasis is on *writing*—not on meditation. I use meditation simply as a tool to start the writing flowing.

You've had the speech on the value of using meditation with your writing in the previous chapter. Now here are some specific meditation techniques you can combine with the writing exercises in the following chapters. Most of the exercises already incorporate meditative techniques such as visualization, guided imagery, inner focus and body awareness. But I think you'll find that taking a few minutes to use one of these techniques before you begin an exercise will add even more depth to your writing.

The five techniques outlined in this chapter start with the shortest, simplest one and then progress in length and complexity. All of them are easy to learn and use.

THE PAUSE THAT REFRESHES

This is a short pause of about 1 to 3 minutes, which will bring you into the present and into your body—and it's simple to do.

Sit up straight, hands on thighs, with your back away from the chair.

Fix your gaze on a spot on the floor.

Pay attention to your breathing for a few moments.

Extend your hearing to the farthest sound.

Still keeping your gaze fixed, become aware of things on either side of you.

Become aware of how your feet feel on the floor, how your clothes feel against your skin, how the air feels as it circulates around you.

Keep your gaze fixed and your attention focused until you feel relaxed.

Take several deep breaths and then begin writing.

SPIRAL BREATHING

This is a simple breathing exercise that will help relax your body and open your mind.

Sit up straight, feet firmly on the ground, with your back away from the chair.

Begin by simply observing your breathing. Don't judge it or make any attempt to adjust it. Simply breathe and observe.

Next, imagine that your spine is like a thermometer with a red ball at the base. Breathe deeply and pull the red ball up through your spine. Imagine it circling slowly and traveling all the way to the top of your head.

Hold your breath and visualize it circling several times around your head. Exhale slowly and imagine the red ball dropping gently back to the base of your spine as your breath circles back down.

Exhale fully. Allow a few seconds to elapse in which you are not breathing at all. Then expand your lungs and take in another deep breath and repeat the exercise. Each time you repeat the process, allow your body and mind to relax and let go more and more.

The exhale is just as important as the inhale, and the tendency is not to exhale fully. Concentrate on allowing your lungs to empty completely with each exhale. This releases dead, unused air from your lungs and increases your intake of oxygen—improving both concentration and imagination.

VISUALIZING

Lots of people swear that they just can't visualize. They say they don't see anything when they close their eyes. Actually, your mind never stops producing images, even if you tell it to. If you think you can't visualize, you need to (1) become more aware of the images your mind produces and (2) gain more control of those images.

Here's a very simple technique to help you get started if you have troubling visualizing:

Close your eyes and imagine a large TV screen in front of you.

Project a red rose onto the screen and look at it for a few moments.

Now change the red rose to a purple one.

Then change the purple rose to a yellow one.

You've just visualized—it's that easy. You can practice doing this with other objects such as a coat, an automobile, an umbrella, or a puppy.

Once you've mastered simple visualization, you can gain further practice by doing the following:

Close your eyes and imagine yourself in a beautiful place in nature. See the time of day, the season, and your surroundings. Watch yourself walking slowly through the lovely setting. Observe all the different things you pass as you walk.

Now stop and sit down. Notice what you have chosen to sit close to. Look around and observe what you see from this new vantage point.

Suddenly some activity happens far away from you, but you can observe it from where you sit. Watch what happens closely, paying attention to the sights and sounds that occur.

After the action is over, see yourself getting up and walking back the way you came. Notice if anything has changed in the setting as you return.

You might find it helpful to write down the scene you saw as evidence that you can, indeed, visualize. Practice this exercise often as a way to increase your inner-eye imagination.

FULL-BODY RELAXATION

You'll find this technique useful before you undertake a long writing stint. It takes about 10 to 15 minutes, and the goal is to empty your mind and body of all tensions so that you can fill them both up with new ideas. Don't struggle to stop your thoughts. Let them flit across your mind but don't follow any of them.

Lie down, preferably on the floor, and get very comfortable. Loosen your clothing and remove your shoes. Put a light cover over you if you feel cool.

Close your eyes and begin to concentrate on your breathing. Imagine your breath traveling up and down your body, relaxing it further with each inhale and exhale.

Still your mind by counting each breath, by seeing a piece of black velvet material, or by saying one word (such as "quiet") over and over to yourself.

Start to relax your body by tensing your toes and then letting them go. Then travel up your body—to your calves, thighs, buttocks, arms, shoulders, neck, and face—tensing each set of muscles and then letting them go completely. Try to isolate each area of your body and focus your full concentration on that area. Inhale for 3 counts, hold your breath for 3 counts as you tense, and then exhale for 3 counts.

With your eyes still closed, pick up each part of your body and let it fall loosely back to the floor. For example, pick up your left leg and then let it fall; then your right. Pick up your head and let it fall, your buttocks and so on.

Take your breathing up to the crown of your head and imagine your breath circulating in your brain, clearing out all the worries, fears, and confusions. Imagine a bright light turning the inside of your brain white and empty. Maintain this state of emptiness as long as possible.

After you feel totally relaxed, open your eyes and lie there until the thought of something important to do—or write—propels you to your feet.

REGRESSION

Since much writing requires that we gain access to the past, this exercise is designed to help you remember things you think you have forgotten. It can also help you see minor details more vividly.

Close your eyes and relax yourself with several deep breaths.

Imagine yourself going inward and then far down. You can do this by imagining yourself (1) curling into a soft ball, which bounces down stairs into the basement; or (2) on an elevator, descending toward a dimly lit lower floor (and you can count down the floors as you go); or (3) free-falling into a warm, safe darkness and landing on a soft bed of feathers or grass.

Once you are at a deeper level of feeling and thinking, call forth a picture of yourself at any age. Just think of any age, see what comes up, and take whatever it is.

Stay with yourself at this age for a few minutes and try to recapture how you looked and felt at that time in your life. It will help to remember where you lived and who your friends were at the time, what you wore and the things you liked to do.

Now allow any scene from that age to appear in front of your mind's eye. Look at what is happening very closely. Tune in to all your senses—what you see, hear, smell, taste, and feel. Stay with it until you get the feeling that the moment is actually happening all over again.

Let the scene dissolve and imagine yourself rising back to the surface, back up to reality. You can do this to a slow count of 10. When you come out of the regression, take time to recall all you experienced.

A Word about the Exercises

I detest the word "exercise" and generally run away from anything that sounds like it. So I apologize for naming the things in this book exercises. They are more triggers for writing than exercises; but "triggers" sounds a bit strange, and so did everything else I could think of. Finally I gave in because nothing else would do. They are, in fact, exercises of a sort. They build writerly muscles.

I get ideas for the exercises from things I read and things I do, so the works of other authors gave me sparks for some of these exercises. You'll find some of the authors and their books listed in the back, or if I can trace ideas directly to others, you'll find them listed in the acknowledgments.

All of the exercises grew out of my desire to overcome my own writing blocks and to help my students overcome theirs. I've been developing and perfecting most of them for a number of years and have found that they usually work. The writing that comes out in class when we use the exercises is nearly always vibrant writing full of voice and imagery—quite a break from the usual college compositions. The same is true for the adult classes I've taught using the exercises. Something about them helps people to produce genuine writing that they feel good about. And that's what I'm after for you.

The whole point of the exercises and this book is to move you through short, rapid, varied experiences in order to increase your flow of writing. Then when you feel sparked by a particular piece you've written, you can lengthen it or rewrite it in different ways. Most of the exercises can be done over and over again and will produce entirely different outcomes each time. They are a source book for all sorts of writing—plays, poems, fiction, essays, autobiographies. One exercise may even start you on the road to a major work.

I think of the exercises as warm recipes for a chilly night, something you can turn to for comfort and fuel when you feel cold or dispirited. They will stimulate your inner consciousness and make more material for writing available to you. Doing the exercises is like doing spade work in preparation for planting a garden—they help break up the old crust of habitual thinking.

Each exercise contains some form of meditation, introspection, body awareness, or reliving of past events. You might find some of them to be intense emotional experiences, so go gently with yourself and do only what you feel ready to do at any given time.

I grouped the exercises by what they *do* for your writing. They start at the simplest level—the body—and move progressively deeper through feelings, sensory awareness, mental observations, memories, and imagination. They first tune you in and clear you out; then they open up your senses, and finally take you further inward, into your mind, your past, and your imagination. They all overlap—that's obvious. Almost any given exercise could be grouped elsewhere.

In addition, I've given you two alternate groupings at the end of the book, which suggest ideas for different uses of the exercises. The first group is by subject, such as Childhood, Self-Exploration, Nature. The second group is by writing technique, such as Story Ideas, Creating Characters, Voice. You'll notice that these, too, overlap a lot, but I wanted to give you some alternative groupings so that the exercises could be used as flexibly as possible and perhaps yield different writing, depending upon how you use them.

And now for the disclaimers: These exercises will not save your writing career or get you a fat advance from a publisher—at least not directly. Nor will they cure you of anything. Though they may have therapeutic value, they are not meant to be therapy. They are meant to be *writing* exercises. Anything else that happens is just a fringe benefit.

Comes now the second disclaimer paragraph. This is not a book of writing assignments. You may use it like that; but I want it on record that I refuse to recommend it as such. In the first place, I have a basic resistance to assignments and exercises and I bet you do too. The language of the exercises is necessarily directive and authoritarian, in the interest of getting the steps down 1-2-3. But don't allow yourself to feel pushed and pulled around by them. Pretend you're at a smorgasbord, and pick and choose only what appeals to you. You're in charge here. Do things however and whenever you like.

Also, I have made a deliberate choice to use the third person plural pronoun—"they, them, their"—as a singular pronoun in most of the exercises. I don't love it but neither could I bear to use "he/she" over and over or to randomly alternate pronouns. Either choice would have been a distraction.

I'll end this chapter by making a few overall suggestions for using the exercises:

Keep the flow of writing going immediately after the exercise. Go directly from the exercise into the writing and don't stop to think or take a break. If you find yourself stuck, simply keep writing the word "stuck" or some noncharged word such as "the" over and over. Soon new words will come—just like breathing.

Resist the impulse to go back and read what you've written over and over. Push yourself to skip over your words like a brook moving rapidly. Forget correctness, the "best" word. And forget trying to be a good writer. Get used to being a bad writer if that's what it takes to help you get off your own back and let your writing live.

Above all, *never* use any of these exercises to judge or condemn yourself. This book has magic ingredients and will disintegrate if you do so.

Ways to Use ____
the Exercises

Some of the exercises are long and involved, but nearly all of them can be used in the simplest way. Experiment with what works best for you at any given time. Sometimes you might have the time and psychic energy to devote to doing an exercise in depth; other times you might just want to grab the title, use it as a topic, and take off writing. Often you will find yourself using the steps within the exercise out of sequence and that's fine too. Keep it flexible.

Here are some suggestions on how to use the exercises in different ways.

USE THE TITLE AS A TOPIC

You can simply look at the table of contents and pick an idea without even reading the exercise or going through the steps.

READ THE EXERCISE AND
THEN DO AS YOU LIKE

Going a bit further than above, you can turn to the exercise, read it through rapidly, and use whatever ideas stick in your mind.

USE ONE OF THE
MEDITATION TECHNIQUES
ALONG WITH THE EXERCISE

The five meditation techniques outlined in a previous chapter begin with the simplest 1-minute focusing exercise and include two breathing exercises to relax your entire body, as well as a visualization and a regression exercise. If you're already used to meditation, good. If not, try one or two of these whenever you feel ready. You can do the exercises without using the meditation techniques, but you might find yourself writing from a different place or having a deeper experience if you use one of these basic techniques.

A note about closing your eyes: I know it sounds ridiculous to say close your eyes during the exercise. How can you possibly read the instructions and write the exercise with your eyes closed? But try to close your eyes during the exercise *as much as possible*—whatever you can manage easily. Closing your eyes increases the vividness with which you can see and recall things. With practice, you'll find that you can open your eyes to check out where you are, write a little, and then close your eyes again.

FOLLOW ONLY THE MAJOR STEPS
OF EACH EXERCISE

Each exercise is set up so that you can easily follow only the basic progression. This means you will pass over the additional questions and instructions written underneath and concentrate only on the major steps.

DO EACH EXERCISE IN DEPTH

In addition to reading and following each of the basic steps, you can also read and consider the supporting material beneath each step. This takes longer but will produce more in-depth writing. If you don't feel like doing each step and answering each question, just pick out the ones that interest you and do only those. The questions are meant to evoke additional material, so just do the ones which seem useful to you. Sometimes you may want to do an exercise in full; other times you may want to do a quick writing. Since the exercises are designed to be used over and over, you can try different techniques.

READ THE INSTRUCTIONS INTO
A TAPE RECORDER

An ideal way to approach the exercises is to record the instructions and then play them back when you want to do an exercise. This will more nearly approximate having someone guide you through each exercise and will give you the maximum relaxation. This is not everybody's cup of tea, however, so don't let this suggestion discourage you in any way.

HAVE A FRIEND GUIDE YOU
THROUGH THE EXERCISE

If you have a writing friend, someone with whom you share your work, ask them to read the instructions to you while you close your eyes so that you can really visualize. Then you can return the favor.

DON'T FOLLOW ANY OF
THE ABOVE SUGGESTIONS

My final suggestion is to forget all these suggestions and instructions. Do as you please. Use these exercises any way you want— cut them into strips and mix them all up, scratch out anything you don't like, add your own ideas and instructions, draw wild pictures. Do anything *except* trudge through them like a good little student. These exercises are designed to help you break barriers, so please don't turn them into another noose with which to strangle your writing. Treat them daringly. Make them your own—just as you do your writing.

Part II

THE EXERCISES

——— *Clearing Out* ———

The exercises in this section, which includes "The Body" and "Intense Emotions," are designed to clear out physical and emotional blocks. They will help you release physical tensions and tune out emotional static so that you can take in more of the world around and within you.

THE BODY

> Exactly where you are at this very moment, there is a house that bears your name. . . . That house, the hideaway of your most deeply buried, repressed memories, is your body.

> —THÉRÈSE BERTHERAT
> *The Body Has Its Reasons*

These exercises come first in the book because they work with the primary, most tangible resource you have as a writer—your body. Your body is like a map of your existence—pockets of history, landfills of emotion—and contains clues to every experience and reaction you've had in your lifetime. The exercises will help you add viscera—bodily substance—to your writing. They can also reveal blocks and tensions and help you to work through them. The following exercises are in this section:

A History of Your Nose
Exploring the Face You Know Best
A Body Symptom Speaks
The Chocolate-Covered Cherry Melt
Scars
Dissolving a Kernel of Grief
Recapturing a Feeling of Yourself as an Infant

———— A HISTORY OF YOUR NOSE ————

Each body part has a story it could tell. In this exercise you'll focus on the major events in the life of your nose. Before beginning, take a few moments to take some deep breaths and relax in order to become more tuned in to your body.

Become Aware of Your Nose

Close your eyes and become aware of your nose. Check your breathing to see where your breath moves freely throughout your nose and where it is blocked.

Explore Its Shape

Using your fingertips, explore your nose and really get the feel of it. Feel the bridge, the nostrils, and notice if any memories or emotions come up as you do so.

Recall Your Earliest Awareness of Your Nose

Go back to the earliest recollection you have of being aware of your nose. What caused you to notice it?

Trace Its History

Recall all the major events that happened to your nose.

- ✓ Have you had pains with it—such as accidents or discomforts?
- ✓ Have you had pleasures with it?
- ✓ Can you remember any funny incidents relating to it?
- ✓ What is the biggest event in the life of your nose?

Explore Your Relationship with Your Nose

- ✓ What are your feelings about your nose?
- ✓ How have you used it?
- ✓ What does it contribute to you?
- ✓ How do you treat it?

Write the history of your nose, developing one of the major events in more detail. You can tell it from your point of view or let your nose speak for itself. Add to the history a sketch of your nose and indicate any blockage or trouble spots.

You can use this same exercise to write a history of all your other body parts—such as your feet or hands, your back, hair, tongue, eyes, or genitals.

EXPLORING THE FACE
YOU KNOW BEST

The face in the mirror—you see it every day. But do you *see* it? In this exercise, you'll give yourself the opportunity to study your own face and then write a self-portrait. Read through the directions ahead of time so you can close your eyes when you explore your face.

Look into a Mirror and Closely Examine Your Face

Look at it objectively, as if you had never seen yourself before. Study your features and your facial expressions. You will probably see all your flaws and wrinkles first. Push past them and look also at the pleasing aspects of your face.

Keep That Visual Image in Mind as You Close Your Eyes

Keeping a visual memory of your face with you, sit in a comfortable chair and close your eyes.

With Your Eyes Closed, Explore Your Face with Both Hands

Don't rush through this. This should take a while to experience, so go slowly. You might need to go through each of these steps several times.

- ✓ Begin with your forehead. Run your hands over your entire forehead, feeling the width and height of it.
- ✓ Next, take your hands down to your eyelids, eyes, and eyebrows. Experience shape and texture as you go.
- ✓ Explore your nose—the bridge, the nostrils, the cavities of it.

- ✓ Move your hands across your cheeks and up to your temples.
- ✓ Now move your hands down to your mouth and explore your lips, teeth, and jawline. Don't forget your chin.
- ✓ After you've explored your entire face with both hands, you can use one hand first and then the other to travel back up, seeing how different your face might feel to each hand.

Make a Rapid Sweep Over Your Face and Trace All the Contours

With both hands, trace the contours of your features, just as an artist might. (You can do this with your eyes either opened or closed.)

- ✓ Does your face feel the way it looks to you?
- ✓ What feelings were you aware of as you felt your face?
- ✓ What images did you see?

Return to the Mirror and Examine Your Face Again

Again, don't rush to criticize. Stay objective.

- ✓ Does it look any different to you?
- ✓ Do you see anything you didn't see before?
- ✓ Have your feelings changed in any way?
- ✓ Did you make any discoveries?

Before you begin to write, you might do a little sketch of how you "saw" yourself with your hands. If you were an artist, what kind of self-portrait would you draw? As a writer, how would you describe this face you know so well?

Another way to approach the exercise is to describe yourself using the third person.

Every symptom contains a message. Obviously if the symptom seems life-threatening, we take steps to get rid of both the symptom and the cause. However, we probably all live with mild, chronic body disturbances which come and go at different times in our lives. Some of them disappear; others hang around indefinitely. For this exercise, choose a symptom you feel safe working with. Experiencing extreme fear is not the point of the exercise. Your chances of coming to some resolution or understanding of the symptom are improved if you remain calm and open.

Lie Down and Become Connected with Your Breathing.

Close your eyes and breathe deeply for a few moments. Use the Full-Body Relaxation, if you have the time.

Imagine Your Body Curling into a Soft Ball

After you have taken several of these deep breaths, exhale fully and imagine your body curling into a soft ball. Take yourself right into the middle of the soft ball. Once you are inside the ball, choose one particular physical discomfort you have.

Describe the Symptom to Yourself

Describe the symptom, avoiding all medical terms.

- ✓ What does it *feel* like?
- ✓ What do you imagine it looks like?

See If Any Visual Images Are Associated with the Symptom

If you stay with the sensations long enough, your imagination will begin to produce images. These images can give you important information about the nature of both the symptom and the cause. Stay with this for awhile.

Think Back to When You First Experienced This Symptom

Allow your mind to travel back to when you first experienced the symptom and see if you can remember what was happening in your life at that time.

Return to the Present Images and Sensations

Continue to breathe deeply and just stay still, experiencing the images and sensations that come and go. After a while, ask yourself these questions:

- ✓ What is this body symptom trying to tell me?
- ✓ In what ways is it useful to me?

Visualize Yourself Unfolding and Standing Up Straight

Visualize yourself uncurling from the inside and slowly unfolding outward until you visualize yourself standing straight up. Open your eyes and slowly sit up. See if there are any new sensations surrounding the physical problem.

Check in with yourself to see how you are feeling. Is there any change in the body symptom right at this moment?

Write down all the information you got from the exercise, giving special emphasis to specific information you feel you received from the body symptom itself. If it could speak, what would it say to you?

Practice in this kind of visceral writing can give you new ideas for writing. Many writers have made their reputations on minute descriptions of body functions and sensations.

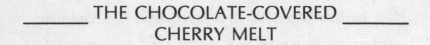

THE CHOCOLATE-COVERED
CHERRY MELT

This exercise is designed to produce maximum mental and physical relaxation and allow you to discover a "surprise" in the center of you. If possible, have a friend read this to you so you can concentrate completely on relaxing. If not, read over the exercise several times before closing your eyes to begin.

Stretch Out Comfortably on the Floor or a Couch and Concentrate on Your Breathing

Lightly close your eyes and breathe very deeply, visualizing your breath coming from the soles of your feet and circling up through your body and out of your head. Do this several times until you feel your body letting go completely.

Visualize a Large Chocolate-Covered Cherry at the Top of Your Head

Try to see a large chocolate-covered cherry atop your head. Stay with it until you get a strong image or a distinct feeling of the cherry.

Imagine the Chocolate Cracking Very Slowly

Visualize the chocolate cracking to reveal a red cherry surrounded by liquid in the center.

Allow the Liquid to Trickle Slowly Down Your Forehead

Allow the liquid to begin running down your forehead and then down your face, totally relaxing every facial muscle as it goes. Take your time. Let the liquid flow as slowly as it needs to in order to relax your muscles.

Imagine the Liquid Inching Its Way Down Your Entire Body

As the liquid flows, it will relax your body completely.

- ✓ The liquid now inches its way down your neck, spreads itself out, and runs down your arms and shoulders. It travels slowly, leaving each muscle totally relaxed and feeling fluid.
- ✓ Still moving very slowly, the liquid continues to run down the center of your back as well as the center of your torso. Feel all the muscles in your spine, your chest, and your abdomen relax as the liquid moves down your body.
- ✓ Allow the liquid to swirl around your buttocks and your genitals, releasing any tension you feel in these areas. Enjoy the feelings of sensuous slowness. Take as much time as you want.
- ✓ Now the liquid flows gently down your thighs, past your knees and shins and onto your feet and toes, removing any tightness or cramping as it goes.

Stay Still and Enjoy the Feeling of Total Relaxation

Lie there for a few moments and explore the delicious feeling of total relaxation in every part of your body. Imagine your body floating in liquid. Nothing is required of you for this moment.

When You Feel Ready, Return Your Attention to the Crown of Your Head

Focus your attention back at the top of your head.

√ What do you see in the center of the cherry now?
√ Has the image of the cherry changed in any way?

As you write down your experiences with this exercise, pay special attention to where most of your concentration was during the process and the different images the relaxation evoked for you. Especially notice what you saw in your "center."

SCARS

The minute you saw this title, a response probably jumped into your head. All of us are keenly aware of our scars. You might have thought of emotional scars or actual physical ones. The exercise is designed to work with a physical scar, but you can also adapt it to emotional or psychological scars.

Make a Mental Run-Through of All Your Scars

You can, of course, make a sketch of your body and put an "X" at every scar site. It's also fine to just scan your body mentally and locate each scar. You'll probably remember a few you haven't thought about in awhile.

Do a Brief History of Each of Your Scars

This can be either a mental or written history. Think about each of your scars:

- ✓ How did you acquire it?
- ✓ At what age?
- ✓ What's most significant about it?
- ✓ How do you feel about it?

Choose One Particular Scar to Work With

You have already done a brief history of this scar along with the others. Now think about why you chose this one to work with:

- ✓ What special qualities does this scar have above the others?
- ✓ Is this a scar you've paid attention to before now?

Remember Back to When, Where, and How You Acquired It

Think more about getting the scar.

- ✓ Where were you?
- ✓ How old were you?
- ✓ What happened that caused the scar?

Put Yourself Into the Moment and Relive It

Close your eyes and go back through the events leading up to the moment of scarring.

√ Who else is involved? What part do they play?
√ What part do you play?
√ What are you doing at this moment?
√ How are you feeling?

Visualize the Scar as It Looks Right Now

Without looking at it, see if you can remember exactly what it looks like.

√ How would you describe it?
√ Has it changed in any way since you first got it?

Take some time to come back into the present before you begin writing. Once you feel ready, recount the incident making it as vivid as possible.
Did you discover anything new about how you acquired the scar? Have your feelings toward the scar changed in any way?

You might have re-experienced some feelings of trauma. Remind yourself that those feelings are related to an event already over and completed in the past.

—— DISSOLVING A KERNEL OF GRIEF ——

Moments of grief, sadness, and loss often stay lodged in our bodies for years. In this exercise, you can let your body lead you to places where you have stored little pockets of grief so that you can begin to dissolve them. Go gently through each of the steps and don't force yourself.

Stretch Out and Allow Your Body to Relax Totally

The more relaxed your body is, the better the exercise will work. Spend a few moments doing deep breathing, spiraling each breath up through your entire body and back down again.

Locate within Your Body a Tightness Associated with Sadness or Loss

Scan your body for tight spots. There will be many different spots, so give yourself time to contact all of them.

✓ Ask yourself the question, "Where do I hold my grief?" Again, many different answers will come, so continue focusing on your body until one spot keeps asking for attention.

Breathe into the Spot and Give It a Visual Image

What does this tightness look like in your mind's eye? The image will probably have a definite connection to one or more of your memories.

Expand the Image

Stay with the image long enough for it to expand.

✓ What other images does it give rise to?
✓ Do the images have anything in common?

See What Memories Are Connected to the Image

Many memories are probably associated with this one spot. Start with whichever memory presents itself to you and then observe any others that rise to the surface.

Choose One Memory and Let It Unfold

Choose the one memory you feel safest working with. Stay with it and watch it from start to finish. As you do so, stay in touch with the tight spot in your body. You may discover that there are other body parts involved.

Re-experience Any Pain and Grief Associated with the Memory

Give yourself over to the memory and do an emotional run-through:

- ✓ How were you feeling as this occurred?
- ✓ Are there other emotions besides pain and grief involved?
- ✓ How is the tight spot in your body connected to the experience?

Examine Any Other Memories Connected with the Spot

After this particular memory fades, focus again on your body and rest awhile to see if there are other memories behind this one. If this memory triggered others, give yourself time to experience each of the other memories and see if they are connected.

Return Again to the Tight Spot and Work to Dissolve It

When you feel you've completed the associations, return again to the tight spot in your body.

- ✓ Consciously begin to dissolve the tightness by putting all your breath into it.
- ✓ Visualize a soft spiral going into the center of the spot and gently opening it up.
- ✓ Take time to consciously release any intense emotions you might still be feeling toward yourself or others because of this experience.

After you've gone as far as you feel you can go in dissolving the kernel of grief, come back to your writing and describe both the memory and your experience of it in your body. You can return to this exercise periodically and continue to work with dissolving this and other kernels of grief.

RECAPTURING A FEELING OF YOURSELF AS AN INFANT

In this exercise, you'll go back to some of your earliest physical sensations and emotions. You may encounter some resistance as you do it. That tells you important material is involved. Be patient, breathe, stay with it.

Lie Down and Do a Complete Relaxation Exercise

Consciously relax your mind and body with whatever method you like. Stay with it long enough to rid yourself of as much tension as possible.

Visualize a Baby's Tiny Body

Call up a picture of an infant in your mind and look closely at how loose and relaxed the baby's body is. Try to match your body to the infant's movements for a few moments.

Picture Yourself as an Infant

You've no doubt seen photographs of yourself as an infant, but if not, imagine what you looked like.

Notice All the Physical Characteristics of Your Infant Self

Closely observe your hands and feet, your head and hair, your stomach, legs, arms, buttocks, eyes, and so forth. What age do you appear to be?

Expand Your Attention to What Is Around You

See if you can visualize anything happening around you.

- ✓ Where are you?
- ✓ Who is with you?
- ✓ Is anything being done to or for you?
- ✓ If you're alone, can you recall any of your surroundings?

Go Deeper and Recapture Some of Your Feelings

Infants perceive things through their feelings in a direct way because they have no words yet with which to divert the feelings. Try to capture within yourself that nonverbal state of being.

Examine One Dominant Feeling

Now zero in on one particular feeling, the one that seems most intense. Don't be too quick to give a name to it; simply allow all the different qualities that make up this feeling to co-exist at the same time. Trace the feeling slowly through all the many layers.

- ✓ What are the characteristics of it?
- ✓ What do you think is the source of it?
- ✓ In what ways does this same feeling continue in your life?

Experiencing yourself as an infant—even if you feel you are just making up the details—can add a new dimension to your writing. Write out, in as much detail as possible, a description of yourself as an infant. Cover both the physical and emotional aspects. Where does that infant now reside within you?

Another way to use the material is to write this from an infant's point of view. How does an infant see the world?

INTENSE EMOTIONS

Denying one's feelings doesn't make them go away. Nor can one overcome a feeling which is really an aspect of the self.

—ALEXANDER LOWEN
Fear of Life

"Negative" emotions—feelings most people would prefer not to have—are easier to use than get rid of. Strong feelings have supplied many writers and other artists with valuable material, and they can do the same for you. These exercises take you back to moments of intense, sometimes painful, emotion so that you can go past any blocks you have and then reshape the experiences in a productive way. This section includes the following exercises:

The Angry Exercise
Early Rejection
Having Your Say
Self-Betrayal
Your Favorite Enemy
Jealousy
A Throw-It-in-the-Fire Confession

THE ANGRY EXERCISE

Anger is probably the least acceptable, least expressed emotion. It's one of the strongest emotions we feel. It's also the one that gets in the way most, blocking other feelings. And we are least apt to be in touch with our anger. You can use this exercise to locate any anger held within you and either clear it out or accept it.

Make a List of All Your Major Angers

Keep asking yourself, "What makes my blood boil when I think about it?" as you write so that you get a full and fairly complete list. Include the following in your list:

- ✓ Things in general that make you angry, including things you identify as "irritations" and "annoyances"
- ✓ Remembered old hurts and griefs
- ✓ Specific incidents in which you expressed your anger.
- ✓ Specific incidents in which you did *not* express the anger you felt.

Choose One of the Blood-Boilers from Your List to Work With

It doesn't have to be the biggest one—just the one you feel like working with right now. It can be a recent or a not-so-recent incident, one in which you expressed your anger or one in which you did not. Just be certain to choose a specific event.

Close Your Eyes and Review the Incident in Which You Felt Intense Anger

- ✓ Where did it take place?
- ✓ Who or what triggered it?
- ✓ What happened?
- ✓ What had happened prior to the buildup of the anger?

- ✓ How did you handle your feelings before and after the incident?
- ✓ What was the final outcome?

Locate the Feeling of Anger in Your Body

Close your eyes for a moment and let the feeling grow as large as it wants to. Re-experience exactly how you feel when you are at the boiling point. Notice all your body changes.

Check to See If You Have Any Unresolved Anger Left

If you still feel anger over the incident of intense anger you just relived, stay in touch with that feeling until it begins to dissolve. Don't turn away from it or talk yourself out of it. If it doesn't dissolve, you might decide to hang onto it a bit longer. That's O.K. You do not have to give up your anger if you're not ready to.

Let the Memory Dissolve and Check into How You Feel

Give yourself some time to see how you feel about your current anger, then think objectively for a few minutes about how you handle anger in general—both your own and someone else's.

- ✓ What are your deepest feelings about anger?
- ✓ How do you act in the face of someone else's anger?
- ✓ How do you usually express your anger?

Write about the moment of intense anger, expressing exactly how you felt then and still feel now. Describe how you feel as fully as possible. Include any insights you may have gained about yourself.

Another possibility for writing is to describe the first time you remember being angry and expressing it on the spot—and how that felt to you.

Each experience of rejection can have a great impact on our lives, especially if the rejection occurred early in life. Through this exercise, you can re-experience an early feeling of rejection and discover how it has affected you.

Go Back in Time to When You Were Much Younger

Using one of the meditation techniques, take yourself gradually back in time to your childhood. Give yourself a few moments to recapture the feelings you had at that particular stage of life.

Locate an Incident of Early Rejection

The incident may or may not have occurred at the age you have gone back to, but more than likely it will have. If not, work with any incident that comes to mind. Think of all the ways we can feel rejected: when we're not given the attention we ask for; when we try to give another person love and they turn away; when someone we care about says mean things to us, and so on.

The rejection can be real or imagined. That is, someone might have verbally or physically rejected you in some way; or you may have simply felt that they were rejecting you. Either experience is fine to work with.

Replay the Incident in Your Imagination

Spend enough time to let all the details unfold, from start to finish.

- ✓ How old are you?
- ✓ Where are you?
- ✓ Who is with you?

Focus on the Moment of Rejection

After you've replayed the incident completely, go back and focus only on the moment of rejection. Expand and amplify that moment as fully as you can. What happened specifically that caused you to feel rejected?

Locate in Your Body Where You Still Feel this Rejection

Scan through your body and find out exactly where you still feel this rejection. Using your body to locate this feeling will help you clarify other memories and feelings that surround the idea of rejection.

- ✓ Is this feeling actually rejection? Could it be something else?
- ✓ What are the main characteristics of this body feeling?
- ✓ Does focusing on this spot recall other experiences with rejection?

Contemplate Your Relationship with Rejection

Ask yourself:

- ✓ How would I describe rejection? What is it?
- ✓ What is most difficult for me about feeling rejected?
- ✓ What have I learned from and about rejection?

Return Briefly to Your Early Incident

Spend a few moments thinking about the relationship of this early incident to your later life.

- ✓ What did I decide as a result of this early rejection?
- ✓ How did the incident shape my future?
- ✓ In what ways is this experience still affecting my life?

Write down a detailed, almost analytical account of your early experience with rejection, and then bring it into the present. Include a description of what you think rejection is. Is it one of the basic feelings? A cluster of other feelings? Also think about what underlies the *idea* of being rejected.

—————— HAVING YOUR SAY ——————

Remember all those times you wished later you had said something but didn't? Now you have your chance. In this exercise, you get to experience what it's like to say exactly what you want to someone else.

Become Aware of Your Throat

Close your eyes and take a few deep breaths to relax your body. Become aware of your throat and any tightness you feel there.

Mentally Assess Your Ability to Say What You Want

Do you usually say what you think or feel? If not, why not?

Visualize the Face of Someone You Want to Say Something To

Imagine the face of someone with whom you have unfinished business, someone you have needed to say something to. Look into the eyes of this person and remember what it is you wanted (or want) to say.

Imagine Yourself Saying Exactly What You Want to Say

Become aware again of your throat as you imagine yourself speaking and notice any sensations such as tightness or excessive swallowing.

Push Yourself to Keep Speaking Until You've Said What You Want

Continue to hear yourself speak as you look into the person's eyes. Even if you think you've finished, push further to see if there's more you want to say that you've been unaware of. Keep going until you feel you're completely finished.

Repeat What You've Said at Least Once

After you've completed what you want to say, mentally repeat it a time or two for reinforcement until you feel totally at ease in speaking the words to this person. You can say this out loud if you feel comfortable doing so.

Return to the Sensations in Your Throat

- √ How does it feel now that you've had your say?
- √ How does it feel when you suppress what you want to say?

Now write down exactly what you want to say, as if you are addressing the person directly in a letter. You might find that you don't need to send it once you've put it down, but you have the option of doing so if you want to.

How does your throat feel after you've *written* what you want to say rather than speaking it?

What have you discovered about yourself in relation to saying what you want?

Use this exercise to exorcise all those times you wish you had said something but didn't. You can also use it for figuring out what you want to say to someone ahead of time.

An alternate exercise could be writing this in dialogue form, imagining the person replying to what you say. Instead of delivering a monologue, you can let the situation develop into a natural give-and-take conversation.

SELF-BETRAYAL

Most of us can recall times when we've felt betrayed by friends, family, lovers. What's more difficult to remember and understand, however, are moments when we betrayed ourselves. In doing this exercise, stand back, observe, and report the event from a distance. The idea of betrayal, especially self-betrayal, can be an emotional hot spot, so don't judge or blame yourself.

Think about Betrayal and What It Means to You

Allow your mind to wander back over the past. Think about moments when you felt betrayed by others.

Think about Times When You Were Unfair to Yourself in Some Way

Go back over various times in your life when you acted disloyal to your self, when you did not stand up for what you wanted or needed, and in that way betrayed your deepest impulses.

Choose One of the Incidents to Work With

Pick an incident to think about. It doesn't have to be a dramatic one, just a moment when you went against yourself in some way.

Relive the Scene as Vividly as Possible

Recreate the moment.

✓ Where are you?
✓ Who's with you?
✓ What is happening?
✓ What has happened prior to this?

Focus on the Moment of Self-Betrayal

Think about the precise moment you betrayed yourself.

✓ How does the moment arrive?
✓ What is going on with you at the moment you betray yourself?
✓ How do you feel at the time?

Get a Physical Sense of How it Feels to Betray Yourself

Think about your body's reaction to the moment.

- ✓ What were the physical sensations you felt during this incident?
- ✓ Have you felt them at other times?

Think about the Aftermath

Ponder the effects of the betrayal.

- ✓ What were the results of this incident?
- ✓ What other choices could you have made at the time?
- ✓ What decisions did you make afterward?

When you're ready to write, get comfortable, take a deep breath, and plunge in. Go easy with yourself.

————— YOUR FAVORITE ENEMY —————

We've all had enemies at one time or another—at least in our minds. Some of these people come and go at different points in our lives. But there are always one or two who walk on the heels of our thoughts wherever we go. We never seem to escape them. Choose one of them for this exercise. The person can be someone who, though perhaps long gone from your life, continues to gum up your thoughts and set your blood boiling.

Put Your Favorite Enemy in Front of Your Eyes

Take a good close look at this person.

- ✓ Do you notice any unusual characteristics?
- ✓ What attracts you?
- ✓ What repels you?
- ✓ How do you think others see this person?

Remember an Incident with Your Enemy

Think back to a time when you felt that this person was opposed to you in some way.

- ✓ What made you decide you were being opposed?
- ✓ What did you feel this person wanted to do to you? Why?

Replay the Incident from Start to Finish

Look closely at both the other person's actions and your own throughout the incident.

- ✓ What part did you play?
- ✓ What did you feel at the time?

Switch Places with Your Enemy

In your imagination, you are now going to take on your enemy's role. When you run the incident through again in your mind, this time you will be doing what your enemy did. Stay with it until you can visualize yourself performing those actions.

- ✓ What are you thinking and feeling?
- ✓ *Why* are you doing this?

Bring Your Enemy Face-to-Face with You Again

Look straight into your enemy's eyes. What do you see there? Say the words you have always wanted to say. Keep going until you get it all out. Don't quit until you've resolved the conflict to your satisfaction.

When you start to write, pay attention to your changing emotions and try to capture each of them as you narrate the event.

Did you learn anything from reliving this incident?

Did your feelings about your enemy change in any way?

Turn your favorite enemy into the villain for one of your stories. Do a portrait sketch in which you portray the person as objectively as possible. Make the character a complex human being with many facets—in other words, create some sympathy for the character while still portraying a villain.

JEALOUSY

Maybe you don't have a jealous bone in your body. If so, perhaps at least once in your life you felt some envy when you observed someone else getting what you wanted or felt you deserved. If you're more comfortable with envy than jealousy, adapt this exercise accordingly, but explore one of those times when you felt intense rivalry toward another person.

Think about the Word "Jealousy" and All the Images It Brings Up

Just think in a general way about the beast called jealousy—commonly known as "the green-eyed monster."

- ✓ What are some other words you associate with it?
- ✓ What scenes come to mind? They can be from your own life, from movies, from books, or from your imagination.

Think Specifically about Jealousy between Lovers

The most common—and probably the most sensational—jealousy shows up in love relationships. Possessiveness, suspicion, infidelity—these are the familiar catalysts for jealousy between lovers.

- ✓ What scenes or stories about others come to mind?
- ✓ What personal experiences come to mind?

Consider Other Common Forms of Jealousy

Move your thinking now to other forms of jealousy (or envy), such as rivalry over sports, jobs, physical appearance, financial success, and so on. Think of the many areas of life and different kinds of activities that are apt to cause jealousy.

Locate Several Instances of Your Own Feelings of Jealousy

Think back as far as early childhood to times when you felt jealous of another person. Make a list if you like.

- ✓ Do you see any common threads?
- ✓ Did you tell others about your jealousy?
- ✓ How did the feelings of jealousy cause you to act?

Focus on One Specific Incident in Which You Experienced Intense Jealousy

The incident can be a big one or a small one. Just be certain that you remember the intensity of feeling surrounding it.

- ✓ Recall all the details of the incident.
- ✓ What specifically triggered your jealousy?
- ✓ Toward whom was your jealousy directed?
- ✓ What was the outcome?

Recall all the Feelings Surrounding the Incident

- ✓ What other feelings besides jealousy were present?
- ✓ Did anyone else know how you were feeling?
- ✓ What were the specific qualities of your jealousy? Describe it fully.
- ✓ What actions did your jealousy cause you to take?
- ✓ Did your jealousy result in any benefits for you?

In your writing, explore the nature of your jealousy as well as the incident itself. Consider the cluster of feelings around jealousy as well as how you experience jealousy. Find new words for this feeling rather than depending upon clichés. Also think about yourself in relationship to jealousy. Have you ever used it constructively? If so, write about it.

A THROW-IT-IN-THE-FIRE
CONFESSION

Here's a chance to write down the one thing you've never confessed to another living soul. Or, if you told someone else about
it, maybe you didn't tell the *whole* truth. Isn't there one important
thing you left out? Didn't you change things around a bit? Don't
worry—no one else will ever see this confession because you are
going to throw it in the fire when you're through writing it.

Contemplate the Nature of Guilt and Confession

Take a few moments to put yourself into a state of reverie. Think
in a general way about the nature of guilt and confession, of
crimes against others. Think about things that have been done to
you and things that you've done to others that you would call
"terrible."

Mentally Examine Your Life

Pick out some of the things you've done that continue to cause
you shame, guilt, or embarrassment. If you think through as much
of your life as possible, some things will occur to you that you
have long forgotten. You don't need to write them down; simply
run them through your mind.

Choose the Incident That Causes You the Most Discomfort

When you feel ready, choose the incident that causes you the
most discomfort. If this upsets you, select an incident with less
emotional charge.

Recreate the Incident

Recreate it by thinking back through every step.

- ✓ Locate the event in time and space.
- ✓ People it with the other actors involved.
- ✓ Dress yourself both physically and mentally as you were then.

Observe Yourself in Great Detail

Go through all your actions very slowly and observe exactly what you felt, did, and thought throughout the event. Explore every inch of what happened as fully as possible, especially the intentions and feelings behind your actions.

Allow the Scene to Fade and Imagine Yourself Alone Seated Before a Fire

Imagine that you are seated next to a blazing fire, alone in a room at a desk. You are writing down your guilty moment in full detail. However, should anyone enter the room, you can immediately destroy this evidence by throwing it into the fire.

Begin to Write Out Your Full Confession

Spare yourself nothing. Force yourself to be completely honest and write down every detail, no matter how nauseating it is to you. Write with the assurance that once you have confessed every detail of your "crime," you will burn it and no one else will ever know. Only you will finally know all the motives, thoughts, and feelings behind what you did.

After you've written out your confession to your full satisfaction, you may find that the event has lost some of its danger and emotional charge. In any case, you are free to destroy what you've written.

You can also turn this into a scene in which a character does exactly what you did. However, just before the character throws it into the fire, the phone rings and they answer it. And—you guessed it—just at that moment, someone else comes along and reads the confession. Then what happens?

———— *Seeing Deeper* ————

This section includes "Sensory Observation" and "Sensory Recall," exercises to help awaken and train your senses. They will intensify your observations of both outer and inner worlds and expand your powers of awareness. Learning to see the tiny details that so often go unnoticed adds truth to your writing.

SENSORY OBSERVATION

POTATO
Inside of one potato
there are mountains and rivers.

—SHINKICHI TAKAHASHI
—*Translated by Harold P. Wright*

"Whatever is before you is your teacher." That's an old saying full of truth. Yet in order to learn the lesson that is before you, you have to first learn to see on many levels—and with more than your eyes. In these exercises, you will have the chance to expand all five of your senses and develop new ways of perceiving things below the surface. The section includes the following exercises:

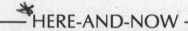

HERE-AND-NOW

We're always hearing about how important it is to be in the moment, to "be here now." But it's not always that easy to do. This exercise will help you focus your five senses on the present moment and open up to what's around you—the quickest way to get right here, right now.

Fix Your Attention on Each of Your Five Senses

Think for a moment about each of the five senses and the organs primarily responsible for that sense. Spend a few moments with each of them and consciously expand their capacity.

- ✓ Eyes—Sight (What do you see?)
- ✓ Ears—Hearing (What do you hear?)
- ✓ Nose—Smell (What do you smell?)
- ✓ Mouth—Taste (What do you taste?)
- ✓ Skin—Touch (What do you feel?)

Make Observations Directly from Each Sense

Work with each sense separately, one by one. Write down what you see, hear, smell, taste, and feel with specific descriptions so that another person could have the same experience you did.

Try to make your descriptions as in-the-moment as possible by actually writing at the moment of experience.

✓ Write 3 to 5 separate sentences for each of the five senses.
✓ Write the sentences in the present tense as if the experience is happening right now.
✓ Locate the experience in time and space.
✓ Use comparisons if they strike you.

Examples:

I see a man in overalls and a red cap, swatting a fly off a gasoline pump.

I hear the soft plunk of widely scattered raindrops as they hit the windshield of the car.

I smell the rancid odor of tarnished metal on the gate—like a smell of rotting onions.

I taste champagne bubbles, which dance in my mouth like a giant puff and then disappear.

I feel the cold, smooth ceramic of the cup against my forehead.

SIGHT Turn off your mental judgments and ideas and just observe what you see. Your eyes will take in many sights without effort. Write down several things that you see—as specifically as possible.

SOUND If you simply relax and allow your hearing to expand, many different sounds will come to you. Again, try to describe the sounds at the moment you're hearing them.

SMELL Breathe deeply through your nose to see what smells come easily to you. Start with these, then consciously choose different objects to smell and describe.

TASTE You'll have to choose items to taste—but they don't all have to be food. You might try out old familiars such as a pretzel, an apple, or sparkling water. Try to write about them at the moment you're tasting them. You can also try out the tip of your ballpoint pen, a flower, a piece of paper, or other things babies routinely put into their mouths.

TOUCH Use your fingers and hands to feel the shapes and textures of different objects around you. In addition, become aware of how the air feels on your skin and the way your clothes feel against your body.

As you use this exercise, you will probably discover that countless ideas for writing surround you at any given moment. To prove this to yourself, use any one of your sentences as an opening for a short essay or story. You can change the tense from present to past if you feel that writing in the present tense is too confining.

———— THE EYE OF THE CAMERA ————

Our eyes record thousands of scenes each day, though we usually don't notice all we take in. This is a visual exercise in which you use your eyes like a camera to record instant photos of simple things you might normally overlook. You'll be closing and opening your eyes throughout the exercise, so read the instructions all the way through ahead of time.

Relax Your Eyes through This Simple Exercise

Before beginning the exercise, relax your eyes by stretching them as you would your arms and legs.

- ✓ Look first to the right, then to the left several times.
- ✓ Roll your eyes in a circle from right to left and then left to right.
- ✓ Look up, then down.
- ✓ Rub your hands briskly together until you feel heat accumulating, then close your eyes and cup your palms over them, allowing the warmth to penetrate your eyes.

Open and Close Your Eyes Rapidly and Mentally Record What You See

- ✓ Keeping your eyes relaxed, lightly open them and then quickly close them again. A good rhythm is *open 1-2-3, close 1-2-3.*
- ✓ Mentally record what you see with your eyes, just as a camera lens would, and then let the shutter click by closing your eyes. Keep your eyes relaxed. Don't reach for the scene with your eyes—just allow it to come to you.
- ✓ When you close your eyes, watch the scene develop on the screen of your inner vision.

Turn Your Head in Another Direction and Repeat the Action

After you close your eyes, turn your head so your line of vision is directed elsewhere and repeat the process of opening and then closing your eyes. Resist the tendency to shift your gaze and look for a scene you like better. Keep your gaze where it lands and click the shutter.

Repeat the Action Several Times

Continue the action of closing your eyes, turning your head, and then opening and closing your eyes again. Do this 6 to 8 times.

You probably won't remember everything you see and that's fine. Without any big effort on your part, your eyes will have recorded several scenes that you'll remember when you start to write.

When you're ready to write about what you saw, keep in mind the following:

In what ways things looked different to you
Any unusual details you noticed
What you observed about using your eyes in this way.

Take time to find the exact words to describe each scene, and try to describe each one from memory. Later you can expand any one of these scenes and use it as an opening for a story.

—————— A PECAN ——————

Establishing a relationship to a small part of nature, such as a pecan half, can illuminate your own nature as well as deepen your connection to Mother Nature. This meditation and the ones that follow, on a flower and a rock, give you an opportunity to observe the many aspects of nature that we often take for granted.

Place a Pecan Half in the Palm of Your Hand

Spend a few moments establishing a relationship with the pecan half.

√ What reaction do you have toward it?
√ How does it feel to hold it in the palm of your hand?

✓ What are your thoughts about it?
✓ What body sensations does it evoke?

Examine the Pecan Half Closely

Look at the pecan half as a representative piece of all nature.

✓ Notice the ridges, the lines, and unusual patterns.
✓ Study its uniqueness; there is no other pecan half exactly like this one.

Turn It Over and Examine the Back Side

Notice how the back side differs from the front.

Break It in Half

Break the pecan in half and study the inside. Note the contrasts between inside and outside.

Imagine the Pecan as It Used to Be

Think about the earlier incarnation of the pecan.

✓ What did the pecan look like before it was shelled?
✓ What was its missing half like? Where is it now?

Put the Pecan into Your Mouth and Eat It

Close your eyes and slowly chew the pecan.

- ✓ What does it feel like in your mouth?
- ✓ How does it taste? Sift through any preconceived ideas you hold about what pecans taste like.
- ✓ How would you describe the taste to someone who had never tasted a pecan?

After you have savored the pecan and feel it integrated into your body, write down what you observed and learned—both about the pecan and about yourself. Notice how much complexity exists in the smallest piece of nature.

Use this same exercise to observe a walnut, a thin slice of kiwi, strawberry, or carrot, a bunch of grapes, or any other natural food.

A FLOWER

Artists draw them and poets write about them. Flowers and their sensuous beauty have excited the imagination of human beings since the beginning of time. We usually see them growing in clumps or grouped in a vase; but a single flower, closely examined, can offer as much pleasure and fascination as a large bouquet.

Choose a Flower That You Feel Some Connection To

If you can find a special flower, work with it; if not, take whatever flower is at hand. Wildflowers make great subjects for observation.

Place the Flower in the Palm of Your Hand

If there are several blossoms on a stem, pick one of the blossoms and hold it in the palm of your hand. Establish some feeling of relationship with the flower. Notice how your body responds to it.

Examine the Flower Slowly and Carefully

Take time to look at every detail of the flower.

- ✓ Look at the petals—their shape and color, the number of them.
- ✓ Study the throat, stamen, and pistil. How are they attached?
- ✓ Look closely for any unusual markings on the flower.
- ✓ Check the variety of textures and shapes in each blossom.
- ✓ Does the flower have a perfume?
- ✓ Study the stem and find out how it is attached to the blossom and to the branch. Observe the leaves.

Consider All the Aspects of This Flower

Think about the different facets of your flower.

- ✓ What is its origin?
- ✓ Where does it grow?
- ✓ How does it grow? (Alone? In clusters?)
- ✓ What speculations can you make about its life cycle?

What Has This Flower Suggested or Represented to the World?

Consider the flower in broader terms.

✓ Has it been adopted as a motif for anything?
✓ Has it been celebrated in art, poetry, song?
✓ Does it have a mythical history?

When you start to write, begin by describing the flower in detail, as if to make another person see it. Even if you don't consider yourself an artist, make an attempt to draw the flower as you see it, noting any unusual characteristics. After you've described the flower completely, you can consider in your writing why you feel attracted to it. Does it hold any memories for you? If you gave this flower a voice, what would it say?

You can use this same exercise with a leaf.

A ROCK

A rock—a hard piece of the earth's crust—something we step on, kick, and curse, is also a thing of beauty which we often stop to admire and collect. Because rocks literally support the very ground we walk upon, they can offer us special knowledge of the earth and our connection to it. If you have a rock collection, that's a perfect place to choose one for the meditation. If not, take a walk outdoors to find a rock for the following meditation.

Choose a Rock from a Group of Others

Pick a rock, and notice your thoughts as you make your selection. Ask yourself these questions:

- ✓ Is this rock worthy of my attention?
- ✓ Why am I choosing this particular one?
- ✓ Is this the one I really want? (Be sure not to settle for one you don't care for.)

Place the Rock in the Palm of Your Hand

Look closely at your rock and take in all its features.

- ✓ Look at the shape of it.
- ✓ Turn it around and observe all the different textures.
- ✓ Test the weight and feel of it in your hand.

Establish a Relationship with Your Rock

Spend a few moments with the rock until you feel a connection with it. In some way, see the rock as an extension of yourself. Does holding the rock in your hand change the way you feel either physically or mentally?

Look at the Rock from Every Angle

Turn the rock over and all around until you have seen it from every angle and have taken in all the variety that it offers. Consider these questions as you examine the rock from all sides:

- ✓ What attracts me to this rock?
- ✓ How is this rock like myself? Are there any physical characteristics we share in common?

✓ How are certain properties inherent in this rock similar to my own unusual characteristics or quirks?

✓ What can this rock teach me?

Write Down Your Observations

Before you begin to write, spend a few moments with your attention focused on the rock. Then make notes or a running commentary as you continue to observe the rock.

After you've written your observations, you might place the rock on your journal, draw an outline of it, and then try to indicate through shadings and drawings the characteristics that seem most important to you. If you want to go further, you can let your rock speak to you and tell you some secret things.

Try this same exercise with a seashell.

—————— A KITCHEN UTENSIL ——————

We generally don't pay much attention to kitchen utensils as we use them; but many of them, when looked at closely, can be as engaging as a work of art.

Choose a Kitchen Utensil to Work With

Choose a utensil that has some aesthetic appeal to you—it can be one you use regularly or one you've never used. An interesting experiment, in fact, is to work with a utensil that you know little about.

Place the Utensil in Front of You on a Table and Look at It Objectively

Take an objective look at the utensil. Turn it around and look at it from all sides. Forget what you know about this object and mentally record what you actually see.

✓ What are some of its features?
✓ What comes to mind when you look at it?

Pick It Up and Get the Feel of It

Hold the utensil.

✓ What kind of material is it composed of?
✓ How does it feel to the touch?

Look at the Way It Is Put Together

Think about how the utensil was made.

✓ Would manufacturing it be simple or complex?
✓ How do you envision it being manufactured?
✓ What are some of its unusual parts?

Reflect on Its Origin

Think about how it came into being.

✓ What was used in its place before it was invented?
✓ Who invented it?
✓ What country does it come from?
✓ Why was it invented?

Think about the Value of This Utensil

Consider the purpose of the utensil.

- ✓ What need does it fill?
- ✓ What gap would it leave if it disappeared from use?
- ✓ What is the relationship between what it costs and the service it gives?

Describe the utensil in complete detail so that someone who had never seen one before could understand what it looks like and how it functions. In writing about the utensil, think about aspects of life that are like the utensil.

You might want to write a poem about this lowly object.

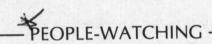

——————— PEOPLE-WATCHING ———————

Each person you see could be the central character in a novel—each of them could tell you a book about themselves. The fine art of people-watching will provide you with many new characters for your own writing. Though this is an "outside-the-house" exercise, it requires that you put yourself into a semimeditative state, a state of mind where you suspend judgment and simply observe.

Go to a Public Place Where You Can Sit Without Interruption

Go to a public place—such as a shopping mall, a train station or airport, a library—any place where you can sit for 30 minutes without interruption.

Sit and Observe the People Around You

Put your judgments aside and simply look at people as they come and go. Keep at it for at least 30 minutes. Take brief notes if you like, but don't get caught up in writing too soon.

Think about What You See

What do you notice when you're not making judgments or trying to make decisions, when you allow yourself to just observe other human beings?

- ✓ How are people alike?
- ✓ How are they different?
- ✓ What are some of the most obvious qualities you observe in different people?
- ✓ What are some of the more subtle qualities?
- ✓ What do many of these people seem to want?

Zero In on One or Two People Who Capture Your Imagination

Think about why they appeal to you.

- ✓ What are some of the characteristics of others that attract you?
- ✓ Do these people remind you of others you know?
- ✓ Could they be characters in a play or story? If so, what roles would you have them play?

Notice Your Own Thoughts and Emotions

Tune into yourself as you sit there observing: How do different people trigger certain feelings in you—such as anger, love, disapproval, pity, envy, pleasure?

Write down your observations as objectively as possible at first and see if you come to any unifying conclusions. Include brief character sketches of the people who most attracted your interest. After that, turn your observations toward yourself and analyze your role as the observer. What did you discover about people in general? What did you discover about yourself as an observer of people? In what ways did you see yourself reflected in others?

———— A PARABLE FOR LIVING ————

Every routine activity has embedded within it a lesson for living. Through closely observing yourself as you undertake regular daily activities, you can gain new insights into yourself.

Choose One of Your Routine Activities

Pick something you do almost by remote control—washing the dishes, pruning a bush, welding, vacuuming, typing, folding clothes, eating, driving your car, taking a shower.

Perform the Activity in Your Usual Way

Spend a few minutes doing the activity in your usual way. If it's not convenient to actually do the activity at this moment, mentally recreate it.

✓ What do you notice about the way you do the activity?
✓ What is happening internally as you do the external activity?

Perform the Activity in a Slow, Meditative Way

Now consciously slow down and put yourself into a different rhythm and frame of mind. Watch yourself as you perform the activity with the expectation that this time it will teach you something about yourself and how you live your life.

Observe Yourself with New Eyes as You Do the Task

Watch yourself as you go through the usual motions and ask yourself:

- ✓ How do I feel as I'm doing this?
- ✓ How is my body responding?
- ✓ What am I thinking about?
- ✓ Am I giving this my real attention? If not, where is it?
- ✓ Am I receptive to what the activity requires of me?

Put Yourself into Harmony with the Activity

Keep your attention on the task that is before you. Adjust your tempo and the amount of energy you're using until you feel you are in tune with the activity.

Open Up Your Awareness to the Lesson

As you continue to observe yourself going through familiar motions, pay close attention to the feelings and attitudes that rise up within you. When you reach a point where you feel in tune with the activity, open up to the lesson it has for you. What kind of personal meaning can you see in how you do this particular task?

Focus completely on the activity and then allow some time to lapse before you begin your writing. In your observation, you might have seen many layers of action beneath a seemingly simple activity. If so, be certain to include a full description of those actions in your writing, as well as what the activity taught you.

SENSORY RECALL

In the world of perception, the present is infinite; the only authority is I, the perceiver.

—CHARLES BROOKS
Sensory Awareness

In the preceding exercises, you used the concrete world and objects that were before you to spark your writing. In these exercises, you will work with sensory recall—using your inner eye to remember and describe places, people, and moments that you have experienced in the past. This section includes the following exercises:

A Moment of Intense Delight
An Eating Experience
In a Crowd
A Place You Know
Someone You Love
Water
Earth
Air
Fire

—— A MOMENT OF INTENSE DELIGHT ——

Delight often occurs in a moment. In the midst of daily life will come unexpected feelings of joy, pleasure, and satisfaction, and the moment then takes its place among our memories. If you feel yourself smiling when you recall such a time, chances are you've hit on a moment of intense delight.

Make a Mental Inventory of Delightful Moments in Your Life

Think of specific times in your life when you were consciously aware of being happy and alive.

Select One of Those Times to Work With

Choose a particular moment to work with. It doesn't have to be a landmark event—just a simple pleasure you've never forgotten.

Close Your Eyes and Relive the Moment

Close your eyes and let the moment expand and envelope you. Put yourself in the middle of it.

- ✓ Where are you? See the physical surroundings in as much detail as possible.
- ✓ Who is with you? Are you alone? With one other person? With several others or in a big group?
- ✓ Take everything in—the activity, the sights and smells, and the feeling within you.

Expand the Feeling of Delight

Focus in detail on the moment when you were aware of the delicious pleasure.

- ✓ Expand that feeling until you can recapture it throughout your body.
- ✓ What is your experience of pleasure at this moment?

Write about the moment in as much detail as possible, keeping your focus entirely on the moment itself so that you can expand it. That is, what led up to it and what happened afterward are not as important as the actual moment. What is the anatomy of delight in your experience?

───────────── AN EATING EXPERIENCE ─────────────

Food. Sometimes we love it; sometimes we hate it. Sometimes it's our friend; sometimes our enemy. But like it or not, we all have to eat it. And many of our moments with food are indelibly inscribed in our memories.

Take a Few Minutes to Relax and Then Focus on Your Stomach

Take a few deep breaths, relax, and tune into the sensations in your stomach—how it feels when it's empty; how it feels when it's full; and how it feels right now.

Do a Quick Review of Your Relationship to Food

Think back over your life and the different feelings and attitudes you've had toward food. Take time to pinpoint any changes you've made in these attitudes over the years.

Visualize the Last Thing You Ate

What did you last eat and when? Visualize it fully. See yourself eating it, paying attention to the texture, the smell, and the taste.

- ✓ How did it feel in your mouth?
- ✓ How did it feel going down your throat?
- ✓ How did it feel in your stomach shortly after you ate it and then much later?
- ✓ How was this alike or different from the way you usually feel after eating something?

Take Yourself Back to a Truly Memorable Experience You Once Had with Food

After you've gotten a sense of your relationship with food, think of a memorable eating experience. The experience can be one you enjoyed or one you disliked.

- ✓ Locate the experience in time and place. If you're with others, put them into the picture.
- ✓ Place the food in front of you and recapture the experience. See the colors, the textures, and how it is served.
- ✓ Imagine yourself tasting it once again. Think of words to describe exactly how it tastes.

In your writing, take the time to give a detailed description of the experience and conclude with why it was so memorable for you. Was this experience characteristic of your usual relationship to food?

Some people flourish in crowds; others shrink away into nothingness. Some crowds are fun and others are torture. Think of the many places you've been where there've been big crowds of people: a rock concert, a packed airplane, a convention, a demonstration, perhaps even a funeral. This exercise gives you a chance to re-experience how you feel about crowds in general and about one crowd in particular.

Close Your Eyes Briefly and Imagine Yourself in a Crowd

Visualize a crowd with your eyes closed. If you can't remember an actual time when you were in a crowd, make one up.

- ✓ Listen to all the things people are saying. Catch fragments of dialogue.
- ✓ Observe how the crowd is acting generally. What word would you use to describe it?
- ✓ Notice specific people and what they are doing.

Check In with Yourself

Think about how you feel about this crowd.

- ✓ How are you feeling while among these people?
- ✓ What major thoughts go through your head?

Think Objectively about How You React in a Crowd

Examine your feelings about the crowd.

- ✓ What is your primary feeling when you're in a crowd?
- ✓ Under what circumstances does this feeling change?
- ✓ How do you usually act? How would you like to act?

Write an analysis of yourself in a crowd. You can start with a crowd you don't like and then go on to one you do like. Look at it from both sides: How you feel when you're on the outside and how you feel when you're part of the "in" crowd.

Then try a purely objective piece in which you describe what you saw and heard. Bring to life some of the people you saw and some of the conversations you heard.

Another idea: Next time you know you're going to be with a crowd of people, plan ahead of time to do this exercise.

—————— A PLACE YOU KNOW ——————

Grandma's house, a beaver dam, a favorite restaurant, your bedroom—particular places like these are sometimes filled with significance. Often a place can become as alive as a human being.

Take Yourself to a Place You Know Well

Imagine yourself traveling safely through dark space. Suddenly you land in the middle of a place you know well, a place you have long loved.

Walk Slowly throughout the Place

If the place is a house or building, go through all the rooms and notice what's in each of them. If the place is an exterior land-scape, walk through every area of it, looking at each thing you pass.

Observe Every Different Part of It

Look for the normal, expected elements of the place as well as anything that distinguishes it. Do you see anything you've never noticed before?

Open Up All Your Senses

Using all five of your senses, record the colors and shapes, the textures, the sounds, smells, and tastes—if any.

Observe Yourself While in This Place

Now turn your attention on yourself.

- ✓ How do you feel when you're here?
- ✓ What makes it so special to you?
- ✓ Do you see other people with you? If so, who are they?

In writing, describe your place in such detail that another person might see it exactly as you do. Take the time to develop all the physical aspects of the place and then explain its significance for you. How would you characterize the "life" of this particular place? Has it influenced you in any way?

Because we are usually so close to the people we love, both physically and emotionally, we often forget how to look at them objectively, as they might appear to an outsider. This exercise gives you an opportunity to step back and take a fresh look at those you love—and perhaps even turn them into characters in your writing.

Form an Image of Someone You Love

Once you've decided on someone, close your eyes for a moment and put the person on your mental TV screen.

Slowly Look Them Over from Head to Foot

Begin by looking at them physically from every angle:

- ✓ See them in a full-body shot, then zoom in for a close-up of particular body parts, and finally end with a close-up of their face.
- ✓ Look for any unusual physical characteristics, especially features that distinguish them from others. Take time to look closely at these unusual physical aspects.

See Them in Action

Let them move about on the screen and observe them in a familiar action. Watch how they walk, run, sit, and so on.

Move in for a Close-Up of Their Face

Go back to a close-up of their face. Let them talk to you, and listen closely to what you hear. If you want to ask them a particular question, do so and let them give you an answer.

Look directly into their eyes for a while and study the eyes in detail.

- ✓ What do you see in those eyes? What are the real feelings behind them?
- ✓ Do you see anything you've never seen before?

Observe Them with Other People

Next imagine them interacting with others—it can be with a group of people or just one other person. How do you think other people see this person?

While you're watching them with others, think about these additional aspects and characteristics of the person:

- ✓ Physical mannerisms
- ✓ Habits of thought
- ✓ Speech patterns
- ✓ Temperament
- ✓ Attitudes

As you begin to write, keep this person you love in front of you, either mentally or by using a photograph, to help you keep your focus.

Describe the person fully, as if you're explaining what they're like to a perfect stranger. Cover all the aspects you saw in the exercise.

This and the three exercises which follow focus on your relationship with the four essential elements—earth, air, fire, and water.

All of us began our lives surrounded by water in the womb, and no other element is as necessary for our physical and psychological survival. Who has not experienced the soothing effects of a hot bath or the blessings of cool water on a parched throat? But not all water experiences are pleasant ones. Some of us have battled for our lives in the depths of rivers and oceans. This exercise gets you thinking about water in general and then zeroes in on a particular experience.

Allow Different Images of Water to Come into Your Mind

Reflect on the many different forms of water that you know: a waterfall, a glass of water, a river, rain, water in a bathtub, ice cubes, melting snow, and so on. Spend time visualizing many different forms of water and their particular characteristics.

Think about All the Ways We Depend on Water

Consider all the ways we use water and are dependent upon it.

- What are the many different ways we use it?
- What happens when there is either too much or not enough?
- What symbols and rituals are associated with it?

Recall Some of the Characteristics You Associate with Water

What adjectives and comparisons come to mind when you think about water in all its different forms?

Think about Your Own Relationship to Water

Think about water in terms of yourself.

- ✓ What is your favorite form of water?
- ✓ What does it do for you?
- ✓ Is there any form of water that frightens you?
- ✓ How would you characterize your relationship with water?

Relive a Few Experiences You've Had with Water

Briefly run through some of your experiences with water. (They can be either pleasant or frightening moments.)

Choose One of These Experiences to Remember in Detail

Pick one of your experiences with water to work with.

- ✓ Where are you?
- ✓ When is it?
- ✓ Who is with you?

Relive the Experience Completely

Think about your experience in detail.

- ✓ From start to finish, what happened? Slowly relive every moment you can remember.

✓ What effect does the water have on your body?
✓ What thoughts and feelings go through you?

Write about why this experience with water stands out in your mind. Recapture the qualities of this particular water and the nature of your relationship to it. Did this event change your relationship with water in any way?

You can also explore the symbolic nature of water—how we have used it in rituals and what it represents to people.

———————————— EARTH ————————————

For this exercise, think about earth not as a vast planet but as the ground we walk upon. When we speak about being grounded, we're generally referring to the quality of being firmly rooted to the earth beneath us—solid, in contact with our bodies and reality.

Spend a Few Minutes Thinking about the Ground You Walk Upon

Recollect the many different kinds of earth you remember seeing. Notice how the qualities differ from one kind to the other. Think about how the ground looks in different situations and places, such as in an earthquake, an excavation, a garden, a fertile plain, a rocky mountain.

Let Images of Other Forms of Earth Come into Your Mind

Let your mind drift through various images of dirt and earth, such as a dug grave, a terrarium, a potted plant, mud pies. Stay with these images until you've covered many different forms in your mind.

Consider the Importance of Earth to Us

Think about how we use the earth.

- ✓ What are some of the ways we use and depend on it?
- ✓ What are some of its physical properties?
- ✓ What are some of the symbolic ways we think of it?

Consider Your Personal Relationship to the Earth

Think of how you react to the earth.

- ✓ Do you usually have much contact with it?
- ✓ When are you most aware of it?
- ✓ How does your body feel when it's in contact with the earth?

Recollect One Memorable Experience You've Had with the Earth

You've no doubt had many moments when you were particularly aware of the earth. Pick one time to work with.

- ✓ Where are you? What is significant about the location?
- ✓ When is it? Think back to right before and right after the moment.
- ✓ Who is with you?

Relive the Experience Completely

See all the details of what happened.

- ✓ What is significant about the moment to you?
- ✓ How are you feeling both physically and emotionally?

Take time in your writing to give the full details, not only of the external events, but of what was happening inside of you. You can include in your writing the different aspects of your relationship with the earth—what it means to you, how you use it.

Another piece of writing might contrast the way the natives in a particular country view the earth—the ground they walk on—and how that changes once other people come into their territory.

AIR

The air we breathe—nothing could be simpler or more taken for granted. We hardly notice the constant circulation of this vital element until it becomes scarce, polluted, or violent. This exercise takes you through some of your subtle—and perhaps not-so-subtle—experiences with it.

Notice the Air That Is Around You Right Now

Sit very still and become aware of the circulation of the air around you. You can do this with your eyes either open or closed, but take enough time to feel the subtle changes in the air as it circulates around you.

Think of Your Relationship to Air

Consider how you interact with air.

- ✓ When are you most aware of it?
- ✓ Have there been times when you didn't have enough?
- ✓ Do you take in enough regularly with your breathing?
- ✓ How does your body feel when you take in either too much or too little?

Reflect on the Different Forms of Air

Think about the visible manifestations of air: for example, light breezes, hurricanes, storms, tornados. What is the difference in experience between feeling the air and seeing it in action?

Choose One Memorable Experience You've Had with Air

Think about one particular experience you've had with air. (The experience can be either pleasant or frightening.)

- ✓ Where are you? Pay special attention to your surroundings.
- ✓ When is it?
- ✓ Who else is with you?

Focus on the Most Important Moment

Relive all the details of what happened. Then focus on the most important moment.

- ✓ What is most significant about this moment?
- ✓ How do you feel physically and emotionally?
- ✓ What happened afterward?

This writing is probably going to be quite subtle because experiences with air are not so readily examined. Stay with it until you get down both the quality of the air and why you still remember the experience.

Another way to write about your relationship with air is to examine your breathing—the way you take in the air that keeps you alive.

FIRE

Fire is endlessly fascinating to watch, dazzling in its beauty, and horrifying in its ruthlessness. It can cook your food or burn down your house; it can warm you or scorch you. Most of the time, you can tame it for your use . . . but sometimes you can't. This exercise takes you into some of your experiences and feelings about this irresistible element.

Think of the Many Different Forms of Fire

Visualize different forms of fire, such as a gas cooking flame, a fireplace, a candle, a match, a blazing forest. Concentrate on the fire itself (rather than the smoke) and get a sense of how these forms differ from each other in appearance.

Reflect on the Many Uses of Fire

Think of all the ways we use and are dependent upon fire.

- ✓ What are the practical uses of it?
- ✓ What are the ways we use it symbolically?

Consider the Different Characteristics of Fire

Note the distinctive traits of fire.

- ✓ What words do you associate with fire?
- ✓ What particular characteristics?
- ✓ What are some common metaphors taken from fire?

Analyze Your Own Relationship to Fire

Pay attention to your feelings about fire.

- ✓ How do you feel in general about it?
- ✓ In what contexts do you enjoy fire or fear it?
- ✓ Where in your body do you sometimes feel fire?

Recall Some Experiences You've Had with Fire

Think back to your experiences with fire. (These can be either pleasant or frightening moments.) Briefly relive any moments in which fire played a big part.

Choose One of These Experiences to Work With

Pick one experience to explore in detail.

- ✓ Where are you?
- ✓ When is it?
- ✓ Who is with you?

Go Through the Experience from Start to Finish

Relive this particular experience. Take each moment and examine it fully.

- ✓ What is your relationship to fire at this moment?
- ✓ What effect is the fire having on you?
- ✓ What are you thinking and feeling?

Write about this experience with fire—why it stands out in your mind and how the experience affected your relationship with fire.

You might also write about the general nature of fire—what it is, how it is used, both practically and symbolically, and how we live in relationship to it. An interesting essay might be to trace a particular type of fire—say candles or outdoor cooking—from the present back to its beginning.

—— *Pushing Beyond* ——

These exercises are designed to push you beyond the boundaries of your usual thinking, remembering, and imagining. This section, which contains "Mind Play," "Memory," and "Imagination," has the greatest number of exercises, because pushing beyond boundaries is an essential ingredient for any artistic creation—including writing.

MIND PLAY

There is nothing either good or bad, but thinking makes it so.

—SHAKESPEARE
Hamlet

Mind play is not only fun; it also expands your thinking powers. In these exercises you'll have a chance to give your mind a workout. Some of the exercises will help you gain greater concentration and inventiveness; others will help you see things in a new way. The following exercises can be found in this chapter:

Synchronicity
Repeat Performance

A Time When You Foresaw the Future
Instant Replay
A Seven-Year Inventory
15 Minutes under the Microscope
Imitating a Favorite Author
A Book Recalled
A Concentration Exercise
Dreaming Up an Invention

———————— SYNCHRONICITY ————————

"Synchronicity" usually refers to events that occur simultaneously. But the word can also be used to describe events that operate in some kind of unison, even if they don't happen at the same time. In this exercise, you will take loosely related events and, through your own observations and connections, turn them into a synchronic happening.

Think of a Time in Your Life When Several Events Took Place That Seemed to Be Unusual Coincidences

Try to remember a set of coincidental events. The events don't have to be big; they can be simple things (such as a certain person, a particular object, a parallel time) that seem connected with some kind of personal meaning for you.

Focus on Each Event Separately

Review in your imagination exactly what happened in each event.

- ✓ How many separate events were there?
- ✓ When and where did each event take place?
- ✓ Who were the people involved in each?
- ✓ What happened in each separate event?

Focus on the Connection between the Events

The events could have happened at many different times, but as you go over them, search for the connecting link between them. The connection doesn't have to be based in objective reality; it can be your own subjective connection.

- ✓ How much time lapsed between the events?
- ✓ In what ways were the different events parallel?
- ✓ What kind of meaning tied them together in your mind?

Think Back to When You First Saw the Connection

When and where did you put the events together in your mind? Be as specific as possible about how this happened.

Review the Events Again and See Them Objectively

This time, look at them from the point of view of an objective observer.

- ✓ How would someone else view this series of events?
- ✓ What would you tell them that would help them see the connection?

Write about the separate events and their connection in a way that would persuade someone else that they were linked. Since the events had meaning for you, your job is now to become the unifying observer and to reveal the exact nature of that meaning—to show why these events could be called synchronic.

REPEAT PERFORMANCE

How often have you found yourself saying "I should have . . ." or "I wish I had . . ." or "If only I'd known . . ."? A common human trait seems to be regret for past actions that we might call mistakes. And coupled with this regret is often a desire to rewrite the past. If you have just such an event in your own life, this exercise will give you the opportunity to make it turn out exactly as you wish—and perhaps finish with it once and for all.

Select an Event in Your Past That You'd Like to Change

It can be a dramatic event—something with a strong emotional charge—or a minor event which, for some reason, keeps replaying in your memory for a reason you might not understand.

Replay the Event in Your Imagination

Close your eyes for a few moments and let the event unfold, from beginning to end, in your mind's eye.

- ✓ Where does it take place?
- ✓ Who are the people involved? Is anyone missing who had an impact on the event?

- ✓ What is your role in this event? What are your thoughts and feelings?

Allow the Memory to Dissolve, and Think It Through Again

Open your eyes and consciously run through the process briefly so that all the details are arranged firmly in your mind.

Start the Event Over and Rewrite the Ending

Visualize the event again. You are now in charge and will rewrite the ending of the incident to suit yourself.

- ✓ Watch the action closely as it progresses. Try to pinpoint the moment that could change the outcome. There may be several points, so mark each of them.
- ✓ When the action gets to one of the turning points, interrupt the action and send it in the direction you choose. Keep doing this until you feel you have events going the way you want them to go.
- ✓ Let the action continue until you reach the full resolution you want. Keep going until you feel completely satisfied.

Review Both Endings and Note How They Differ

Compare the endings.

- ✓ When you put the two endings side by side, how widely do they seem to differ?
- ✓ What was the main pivotal point at which the ending could be changed?
- ✓ Does changing the ending make a small or an enormous difference?

See How You Feel after Rewriting the Event

You may have many different feelings surrounding this event and some of them could be very intense, so take a moment to return to the present and check in with yourself.

- ✓ Did you discover anything new?
- ✓ How did your feelings change when the ending changed?
- ✓ How do you feel now?

When you write, relate the event twice, detailing both endings and how they are different. Or concentrate on the new ending you created and the feelings your rewrite has evoked in you.

Rewriting endings is a great way to stimulate your imagination. Use this exercise as a guide to rewriting the endings of historical events, novels, movies, fairy tales. If you watch soap operas, you can have some fun rewriting each day's episode to your liking.

A TIME WHEN YOU FORESAW THE FUTURE

You can foresee the future in many ways: through dreams, hunches, direct premonitions, gut-level feelings, signs, or even through a voice in your head that gives you prior warning. Getting a glimpse of the future is not exactly like a conscious prediction. Sometimes you don't even realize until later that you foresaw an event which eventually came to pass.

Recollect a Time When You Foresaw the Future

Think about a time when you predicted something that later occurred. It can be something as simple as having a hunch that someone would call or as dramatic as having a prior warning of a major event.

Recreate the Event That Occurred in Full Detail

Note the circumstances of that time.

- ✓ Where did the event take place?
- ✓ Who were the people involved in it?
- ✓ What part did you play in it?
- ✓ What happened? (Trace the event chronologically from start to finish.)

Trace Your Steps Backward from the Event to the Moment of Foreseeing It

Note how you felt when you had your premonition.

- ✓ Where were you?
- ✓ What were you doing at the time?
- ✓ How did the foreseeing occur—what form did it take?
- ✓ How much notice did you take of this foreseeing?
- ✓ What were your feelings at the time?

Contrast the Premonition with the Event

Take a look at the moment of foreseeing and contrast it with the event itself.

✓ How were they alike?
✓ How did they differ?
✓ What was the most unusual aspect of what happened?

As you write, concentrate on the connection between the moment of foreseeing and the actual occurrence. What did you learn from this experience? What impact did this experience have on you?

You can also try your hand at doing some futuristic writing. Pick one small aspect of today's world and let your imagination go. Describe how you think that one aspect will be different in 20, 50, 100, or 1,000 years.

--------------------- INSTANT REPLAY ---------------------

Sometimes past events that you consider insignificant can replay over and over in your mind for no good reason. Your memory bank might bring up at random intervals a scene you saw, something someone said to you, or a simple action you engaged in. Perhaps it's time you took a look at one of these seemingly insignificant events to see if there's anything behind it.

Take Time to Think about the Scenes That Keep Replaying in Your Mind

You may not have any trouble in calling forth some of these insignificant events. But if you do, take your mind back to a day or so ago and trace all of your actions during that day. As you see yourself doing things, try to remember some of the thoughts that were going through your mind. Chances are good that one of these events presented itself to you.

Select One of the Events to Look At in Depth

Choose one of these events. It may have occurred in reality or may be a scene from a movie, a dream, or a daydream.

Close Your Eyes and See the Event Replay Itself

✓ Where does it take place?
✓ Who are the people involved?
✓ In what way are you involved?

Open Your Eyes and Think about the Replay

✓ This time, did it change in any way from its usual replay?
✓ Are there other versions of it? If so, how many?

If There Is More than One Version, Examine the Differences

✓ Which version replays the most?
✓ What difference strikes you as being the most unusual or important?

Analyze Your Role in the Event

✓ What was your actual part in the event?
✓ Do you consider your part major or minor?
✓ How were you affected by what happened?

Think about Other Circumstances Surrounding the Event

Place the event in perspective.

- ✓ What happened before the event? Afterward?
- ✓ What connections or associations does it have to other events?

Speculate on Why the Scene Keeps Coming to You

Take a few more minutes to think further about what happened and ask yourself these questions:

- ✓ Why do I still remember this?
- ✓ Is there something important in this for me?

You might write first about yourself in relationship to the scene in order to discover a possible hidden message. If the scene changes, or if you have consciously altered it, that's also important to record.

You could also start out by describing the event as if it were a scene in a movie, and then allow it to take off in its own direction. It may be a story that wants to get told and keeps replaying in order to get your attention. This is often the way characters come to writers—over and over, demanding that their stories be told.

─── A SEVEN-YEAR INVENTORY ───

The expression "seven-year itch" no doubt sprang from the fact that every seven years we shed our old skin and get a new one, and it has become a metaphor for the instinct to move on—to get out while we're ahead or before boredom strikes. Although we can't always meet this ideal, life still has a way of arranging events so that we experience a natural cycle of beginnings and endings. For this exercise, you'll do an inventory of your life for the past seven years—or for any seven-year interval. (You can also use five, ten, or whatever number feels natural to you.)

Trace One Interval in Your Life through an Entire Cycle

Choose one interval in your life that covers seven (or any other number) years. Make a list of all the major events that took place during this period. Draw a graph to go with it if you like.

Expand Each of the Major Events with Added Details

Jot down additional details about each event: who, what, when where, how, and your perceptions and feelings about the event.

Put the Inventory into Some Kind of Narrative Form

Your written narrative can be short or long, but develop it with enough details so that, as you write, new information will occur to you. What was the major theme of this cycle?

Choose One of the Events from This Period and Describe It More Fully

Take one of the events from your narrative and expand it with more details. See how it fits into the seven-year cycle.

- ✓ How is it related to all the other events from this period?
- ✓ Why does it stand out?

Complete the Inventory by Considering How Many of the Following Phases Are Apparent in Your Seven-Year Cycle

Break your cycle down into specific periods:

Initiation—The activity begins.
Flowering—You blossom and reap the benefits.
Pinnacle—You peak and have gone as far as you can.
Decline—The cycle starts down.
Transition—You move on and begin a new cycle.

Conclude your writing by reflecting on what you've learned about yourself and your life through thinking about it in cycles. This is a good way to write your autobiography or a family history.

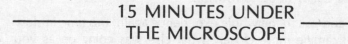

15 MINUTES UNDER THE MICROSCOPE

On the surface, this is a simple exercise: You will examine yourself doing something that takes about 15 minutes. However, as you look closely at these 15 minutes, you will discover layers and layers of complexity—probably enough material to warrant a small novel. If you're familiar with the writings of William Faulkner, Virginia Woolf, and James Joyce, you'll recognize the technique.

Mentally Recount All the Things You did Today or Yesterday

Think back over your day and mentally recount all the things you did. (You can go back to an earlier day, but choose a recent time.)

Pick One 15-Minute Segment from That Day

Choose one segment of your day in which you were doing something that took about 15 minutes.

Close Your Eyes and Visually Recreate the Experience

Put a beginning and an ending to the segment and observe yourself in action from start to finish.

Rerun the Event in Slow Motion

Go back and watch the whole experience again, this time in slow motion. Examine more closely what else was going on as you progressed through the 15 minutes.

- ✓ See each action as completely as possible.
- ✓ Pay attention to the transitions between actions: What prods you to finish one action and begin another?
- ✓ Notice what else is going on around you that is outside your frame of reference but which you still observe.
- ✓ Tune in to how your body is feeling.

Go Back Once Again Through Each Movement and Trace Each of Your Thoughts

Go back through each movement once again. This time, trace each thought you're aware of as you undertake the different actions. You now have a dual mental screen—one for your external actions and one for your internal thoughts.

Slow Down Time Even Further

Slow down time until you are looking at each mental and physical event as if it took much longer to transpire than it actually did. Mentally record every turn of thought and feeling that you can remember. You may have to rerun the scene several times in your mind's eye in order to uncover everything.

Once you've completed the exercise, spend enough time writing to get down everything that you remembered. As you're writing, you will probably remember other things, so add them in.

A good follow-up exercise is to take any one of the threads of thought that ran through your mind and let it write its own story.

—— IMITATING A FAVORITE AUTHOR ——

Studying excellent writers can do wonders for your own writing. In fact, one of the best ways to get variety into your writing is by imitating the sentence rhythms of some of your favorite authors. You can do this exercise any time you're sick of the sound of your own voice and feel stuck in the same old sentence patterns.

Choose a Short Passage from the Works of an Author You Like

The passage should not be long—ideally, one good paragraph.

Study It Closely

Notice any unusual techniques the writer uses. Pay close attention to the sentence patterns. What makes this a good piece of writing for you?

Read the Passage Aloud a Couple of Times

Reading it aloud will give you the chance to feel the rhythm of the sentences and the sound of the words on your tongue.

Copy It In Your Own Handwriting

You will get the feel of the words in your arms and hands as you write. Copy it over several times if you like and take time to savor each word.

Keep It in Front of You as You Begin a Passage of Your Own

Begin your own passage of writing, using your author's sentences as patterns. Don't imitate the words, thoughts, or ideas in the passage. Concentrate solely on matching, as closely as possible, your rhythms and sentence patterns with those of your author.

Keep Going with Your Own Piece of Writing

After you've finished the short imitation, see if you can keep going, moving beyond the imitation into your own creation.

Return to this exercise any time you feel stuck and need some fuel to feed your creative fire. Once the imitation is done, your piece will usually take off in a surprising direction if you push yourself to keep going.

—————— A BOOK RECALLED ——————

To prove to yourself that you know more and remember more than you give yourself credit for, you're going to recall a book you read several years ago—and you're going to do it swiftly.

Choose a Book You Read Once Several Years Ago

Think of a book you read a few years back. Any book will do—it doesn't have to be a long one or a classic. It can be a novel, a biography, or any other nonfiction book. The only constraint is *do not pick one you've seen in movie adaptation.* You want all the images you remember to have been created solely by your own mind.

If Possible, Hold the Book in Your Hand; If Not, Recall What It Looked Like in Your Imagination

Either hold the book or visualize it, and examine it in detail. The physical aspects of the book are important:

- ✓ Was it a paperback or hardcover?
- ✓ What kind of illustration was used on the cover or dust-jacket? Were there illustrations elsewhere in the book?
- ✓ What kind of shape was the book in? Was it new or one used by others, such as a library book or a hand-me-down?
- ✓ Were there notes or other markings anywhere on it? Did you write or underline in it?

Close Your Eyes and Run through the Story Exactly As You Remember It

Try to remember the progression of the narrative with your eyes closed. This is not a quiz on the book. Your memory of the story does not have to be faithful to the book. This is about *the* story *you* got from reading the book. If your book is a novel or one with a story line, run through the plot. If you've chosen a book without a story, run through the sequence of ideas or events as they were presented.

Open Your Eyes and Mentally Go Back Over What You Remembered

Get the story or the sequence of events you've recalled firmly in your mind. At this point you might be agonizing over all you've forgotten. Put that aside and concentrate just on what you remember.

Begin Writing Ideas Down as Quickly as Possible

Without stopping to ponder whether you're being accurate or not, get as much as you can down on paper while it's still in your mind.

Stop Writing and Think Further about the Book

Put your pen down (or stop typing) and think about the book again.

- ✓ What images do you remember most vividly?
- ✓ What part or scene seemed most important to you?

Put Yourself in Relationship to the Book

Think about the book in terms of yourself. What did you bring to the reading of the book?

- ✓ When did the reading take place?
- ✓ Where were you?
- ✓ What was going on in your life at this time?
- ✓ What part of the book moved you most?
- ✓ What was the major idea you got out of the book?

Continue writing now by filling in more details you remember about the contents of the book. What still stands out for you? What did you learn from reading the book that made a difference to you?

Do a separate piece in which you make yourself the central character, and describe your life in relationship to the book. Write a scene that vividly shows where you were at one moment while you were reading the book and what was going on in your head as you read. What were you seeing and thinking?

A 5-MINUTE
CONCENTRATION EXERCISE

This exercise will increase your ability to concentrate, as well as improve the depth and quality of your concentration. By commanding your mind to stay focused on one idea for a set period of time, you can improve your mental flexibility and open up pathways in your thinking.

Sit at a Desk with Pen and Paper Handy

Sit up in a straight chair, preferably at a desk, and have pen and paper at hand. Take several deep breaths, and as you exhale, relax your body more with each exhale.

Choose a Small Object That Is Not in the Room to Concentrate On

The object should be small enough to hold in your hands. *Choose an object that is not in the room with you.* The idea is to build up the image in your mind as concretely as possible.

Time Your Concentration Period for 5 Minutes

Set a timer, or keep a clock where you can see it, and limit your concentration period to 5 minutes.

Begin Concentrating on the Object You've Chosen

As you concentrate, *keep your eyes open* and find a comfortable spot on the floor to focus on. Begin to visualize your object in as much detail as possible. Do not write yet.

Take Your Concentration through Three Levels

You don't have to try all three levels; it's better to fully accomplish the first one before moving to the next. However, if you feel that you want to try all three, you can move your concentration from the concrete to the abstract through these three levels:

CONCRETE PHYSICAL CHARACTERISTICS First build up the physical aspects of your object—its shape, size, weight, color, texture. Really look at it and experience things about it you may not have noticed before. What are some of its most distinguishing characteristics?

PRACTICAL ASPECTS OF THE OBJECT Consider the practical aspects of this object.

✓ How is it used?
✓ Where does it come from?
✓ How does it get to us?
✓ Who invented it?
✓ What are all the different ways it could be used?

ABSTRACT CONSIDERATIONS Speculate on the deeper meaning of your object.

✓ Why do we value this object?
✓ How has it changed historically?
✓ What is its place in today's world?
✓ What does it symbolize to us?

Simultaneously Observe Your Own Mental Processes

As you concentrate, notice how your mind works. Pay attention to both the quality and the focus of your concentration. When you catch your mind wandering, bring it back to your object. Make a small mark each time your mind wanders during the exercise so that you can get a concrete idea of how long you are able to will your mind to concentrate. Note whether your mental wanderings were long or short ones. Were you able to quickly catch yourself and return to the concentration?

Begin Writing as Soon as 5 Minutes Are Up

As soon as the 5 minutes are up, begin your writing. You can write about the object itself—all you thought of—and also how successful you were in your concentration.

If you were not able to move from the concrete level through the abstract level, don't fret about it. Just continue working with the exercise until you can do it. You may discover that even 5 minutes of concentration on one idea can be very difficult at first.

Once you've mastered 5 minutes, expand your time until you're able to concentrate for 15 to 30 minutes at a time. You can then take this exercise even further by concentrating on abstract ideas rather than concrete objects. You might surprise yourself with the wealth of ideas such a simple activity can bring forth.

——— DREAMING UP AN INVENTION ———

Probably everybody at one time or another has said, "Why haven't they ever invented a _____?" Usually that statement grows out of frustration over an unmet need. Now you get a chance to invent an item you've always wanted but have never found on the shelves.

Give Yourself a 15-Minute Concentration Period to Recall Any Past Ideas You've Had for an Invention

Keep your eyes open throughout a 15-minute period of concentration but focus on one spot so you don't get distracted. Keep a pad and pen handy. Think back over times in the past when you've felt frustrated because you needed or wanted an object that simply did not exist. Perhaps you had to put together a make-do object in order to get the job done. If several ideas occur to you, pick one to work with and go directly to visualizing the object. If no ideas occur to you:

THINK OF AN ACTIVITY YOU KNOW WELL AND TAKE YOURSELF THROUGH EACH STEP OF IT Go through the action from start to finish and don't leave out any of the steps.

FIND SOME STEP IN THE ACTIVITY THAT COULD BE IMPROVED BY THE USE OF A NEW GADGET If you can't think of a brand-new gadget to invent, think of a slight improvement. How would you explain to someone else the way this gadget or improvement could help?

Visualize the Object in as Much Detail as Possible

At this point you might want to close your eyes so you can see the object more vividly. Keep looking at it in action until you find yourself creating more physical details for the object.

Now See Yourself Using the New Invention

Go through the activity mentally again, this time *with* the object you've thought of. You are now well on your way to inventing a new thingamajig.

Look at the Individual Parts of the Object

Examine the parts of the object carefully.

- ✓ What are they made of?
- ✓ How are they put together?
- ✓ How do they work individually?
- ✓ How do they work together?

What Will This Invention Do for Others?

Think about how the average consumer could use this object.

- ✓ What is its purpose?
- ✓ Who will use it?
- ✓ How will it make life easier for others?
- ✓ What gap will it fill—or what object will it replace?

How Could This Object Be Manufactured or Otherwise Created?

Consider further how this object is made.

- ✓ What are the materials necessary for creating this invention?
- ✓ By what process could it be put together?

Start to Work Rapidly Drawing or Describing Your Invention

You might have made a few notes or doodles on your pad. Now, however, start writing down all you imagined as rapidly as possible. Add any kind of sketch you can manage. Don't worry about being logical or precise. Simply get everything down quickly so that it doesn't evaporate.

Put Your Ideas into a More Organized Form

Once you've emptied your mind onto paper, you can then put the material into a more organized form. Write down, in detail, a description of your invention and all the ideas you have about it. Draw and label the parts. Give it a chance to exist.

- ✓ What would you name your invention?
- ✓ What kind of advertising slogan would you give it?
- ✓ How could others get hold of it and use it?

Although this exercise is primarily intended to increase your creative thinking powers, it's quite possible you will at some point come up with an invention you think is a winner. If you are willing to invest your time, energy, and money in it, there are many societies for inventors where you can find people who will help you develop your idea and make a model of it.

Even if such inventions only stay in your imagination, however, they can be used in your stories. Science fiction abounds in outlandish inventions—and many of them eventually become realities.

MEMORY

I was gathering images all of my life, storing them away, and forgetting them. Somehow I had to send myself back, with words as catalysts, to open the memories out and see what they had to offer.

—RAY BRADBURY
Preface, Dandelion Wine

Each split second arrives, lives its instant, and then travels into memory. Therefore, anything that is not happening right this second is, in effect, already being remembered. Most of the exercises in this book are based on some kind of remembering. But this section is about *memory,* that vast storehouse which provides most of a writer's material. There's the past—all that shapeless material that keeps piling up like snowdrifts in the whirling process of life. Then there's THE PAST—those incidents and moments charged with meaning for us and already shaped into stories by our memory. You can make use of this endless past without being gobbled up by it. Pull it out, a piece at a time, and polish it with meaning. The following exercises can help you retrieve important memories:

The Big Lie
The Forbidden Act
A Memorable Prank
Outrageous Acts
The Biggest Fight
A Nightmare
A Family Legend
Puberty
First Love
A Favorite Toy
Family Snapshot
I Remember

Maybe you've never told a *big* lie in your life. But chances are you've told at least a little one—and maybe even enjoyed telling it. Through this exercise, you'll get to re-experience the pleasures and pains of lying.

Assess Your Attitudes about Lying

Think about how you currently feel about lying.

- ✓ Do you believe in lying? When and under what circumstances?
- ✓ Do you lie frequently? Easily?
- ✓ Have you always had these attitudes? If not, when did they change?

Think about a Recent Lie You Told

Reflect briefly on a small or big lie you've told recently.

- ✓ What was its purpose?
- ✓ Was it alike or different from other lies you've told?

Make a Brief Mental Note of Other Lies You Remember Telling

After you've recalled the most recent lie, go backward and recall other lies that stand out in your memory.

Choose a Lie to Work With

Pick one particular lie. Go back over all the events that led up to the lie.

- ✓ Was it premeditated?
- ✓ What was happening that made you decide to lie?
- ✓ What was at stake?

Relive the Exact Moment When You Told the Lie

Take time to explore how you and your body felt before, during, and after telling the lie.

- ✓ How old were you? Where were You? Who was with you?
- ✓ To whom did you tell the lie?
- ✓ How did they receive it?
- ✓ How did you feel as you told it? Identify as many emotions as you can remember.

Reflect on the Aftermath

- ✓ What happened immediately after you told the lie?
- ✓ Were you ever found out?
- ✓ Did you ever tell anyone that you had lied?
- ✓ Were there any long-range consequences? If so, did you feel that they were justified or unfair?

Write about the lie in such a way that it seems big even though it might have been small; in other words, make the event sound significant in your telling of it.

Include in your writing what you found out about you and your relationship to lying. How have your attitudes about lying been affected by this incident?

——————— THE FORBIDDEN ACT ———————

If you ever did anything you were forbidden to do by some authority—such as your parents or a teacher—when you were young, you might enjoy looking back on it through doing this exercise.

Reflect on Any Incidents from Your Childhood in Which You Defied Some Authority

Go slowly backward through the years and think about some of the times you did things you weren't supposed to do.

Choose One Specific Incident to Work With

Pick one incident from your childhood. The incident can be one in which you either refused to do something you were told to do or one in which you did something you knew you were not supposed to do.

Relive the Event

Locate the event in time and space.

- ✓ Where are you?
- ✓ Who is with you?
- ✓ What's going on?
- ✓ How old are you?

Focus on the Moment When You Decided to Disobey

Go to the center of the event and look in detail at the moment when you made a decision to disobey authority.

- ✓ Was your decision a strong choice to go against authority?
- ✓ Were you influenced by anyone else?
- ✓ What motivated you?

Replay the Event Again

This time when you go over each part of the event, stay aware of your body and how it feels.

- ✓ How did you feel when you were being disobedient?
- ✓ Where in your body do you still feel that defiance?
- ✓ How do you feel about it in retrospect?

When you write about the incident, include your feelings about it then as well as now. What did you learn? How did this incident help shape your present-day attitudes?

Use this exercise to relive other forbidden acts you may have committed as an adult—acts in which you defied your boss, your spouse, or someone you felt had authority over you.

———————— A MEMORABLE PRANK ————————

People love to laugh, so telling about pranks or practical jokes almost always gets them listening. You've probably observed (or perhaps even engineered) some pranks others would enjoy hearing about. The prank might be as simple as taking someone on a snipe hunt or as elaborate as stealing an alligator from the zoo and putting it into a friend's bathtub. Your intention in describing the prank, however big or small, is to entertain your audience with some humorous storytelling.

Have Fun by Musing on All the Pranks You can Remember

You might have been the instigator, a participant, or even an innocent bystander. Enjoy the memory of any that you can remember and feel the pleasure and laughter inside yourself.

Take a Closer Look at One of the Pranks

Pick one of the pranks and run it through your memory again.

- ✓ Where does it take place?
- ✓ Who are the people, animals, or objects involved?
- ✓ When does the prank start?
- ✓ When does it end?

Pinpoint the Funniest Moment

- ✓ Where does the climax of the prank come?
- ✓ Is any new element introduced at this point? If so, what?
- ✓ How are the people involved affected by this moment?
- ✓ How are the bystanders affected by the moment?

Analyze Why This Moment Was the Funniest

Adopt a new perspective now. Look backward: What earlier elements combined to make this the funniest moment?

- ✓ Does some twist in events or action occur?
- ✓ Is there an unexpected element introduced?
- ✓ What enabled the prankster to bring this off?

Speculate on the Nature of Pranks

- ✓ Why do pranks appeal to so many people?
- ✓ What human need do they answer?
- ✓ How does this fit in with your view of human nature?
- ✓ What specific qualities do pranksters usually possess?

Put this prank into writing for others to enjoy. Work with the details and events until you have distilled them down into the essentials so that the "punch" of the funniest moment comes through. In other words, consciously tell it so that it builds to a climax. You can leave it at that—just telling it as a story—or you can turn it into an essay by giving your ideas about the nature of pranks and why they appeal to people, including you. What, in general, are your feelings about pranks?

—————— OUTRAGEOUS ACTS ——————

Some people can get away with more than should be legal. Surely you know a few people like that—maybe you're even one of them. Certainly literature is full of them. Wherever we encounter these people, we're bound to shake our heads in wonder at how they pull off their outrageous acts. "Outrageous" used in this sense means outlandish, beyond what is expected or socially acceptable. Keep it light for this exercise.

Spend Some Time Running through All the Outrageous Acts You Can Remember Witnessing

Think of funny, amazing, or zany things you've seen people do. Stretch your mind and go for the most outrageous act you can think of. This may take a little time. Make a list if that helps. If you can't think of any you remember seeing, jot down some other people have told you about. Maybe you saw an outrageous act on TV or read about it in the news. Maybe you participated in it yourself.

Think about the Motivation behind Such Acts

Spend some time thinking about human nature in general and what prompts unusual behavior.

- ✓ What kind of people usually do outrageous acts?
- ✓ What, in general, motivates them?

Use One of the Acts On Your List to Analyze

If you actually saw an outrageous event happen or if you took part in it yourself, recount it in your imagination. If you only heard about it, envision it happening in your mind.

- ✓ Locate it in time and place.
- ✓ Who are all the characters involved?
- ✓ What kind of person committed the outrageous act?
- ✓ What action took place prior to this?

Examine the Outrageous Act in Detail

Zero in on just the outrageous action itself.

✓ In what specific ways did this action differ from what is usually expected?
✓ What do you think motivated the person to do it?
✓ In what ways was it justified? Did the situation merit it?
✓ In what ways was it truly "outrageous"?
✓ What was the final outcome?
✓ What was the effect on others?

Imagine this event as a scene in a movie or book. Tell it in as much detail as possible, building up to the outrageous act as a climactic moment. Your job is to make it seem as outrageous as possible—don't just tell what happened; *show* it.

A second piece of writing could be about yourself in relationship to outrageous acts. You could describe some of your own or fantasize about the ones you've always wanted to commit.

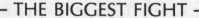

THE BIGGEST FIGHT

Even the mildest and most timid of us have had at least one big, memorable fight. It may not have been an actual fistfight—a loud shouting match counts.

Think of Conflicts You've Had with Others

Think of the major people in your life with whom you've had conflicts—either ongoing or off and on. Identify the underlying reasons why you have felt provoked into conflict.

Think about How You Usually Act When You're Angry with Someone

Think of a time when you felt anger or rage at someone and kept it in rather than expressing it. Then think of a time when you were furious and did not hold it in—a time when your anger flooded out of you and onto someone else.

Choose an Incident to Work With

By now you should have come across an incident you can work with. If it's not *the* biggest fight, it's still something you can use for the exercise.

Set the Scene of the Fight

Put yourself into the scene you have recalled.

- ✓ Where are you? What are the surroundings like?
- ✓ Who is with you?
- ✓ Where were you before this?
- ✓ What had happened prior to this?

Let the Fight Unfold

Go through all the details you can remember that led up to the confrontation.

- ✓ What are you saying and doing?
- ✓ What is the other person saying and doing?
- ✓ Is this person someone you've had other conflicts with before?
- ✓ What are your feelings right before the eruption?

Observe Yourself in the Middle of the Fight

As you put yourself right into the middle of the fight, keep your observations about yourself as keen as possible.

- ✓ How are you acting?
- ✓ How are you feeling inside? (Catalog as many feelings as possible.)
- ✓ What did you want from this person and could not get?

Take the Fight All the Way to the End and Beyond

- ✓ What was the pivotal moment? Could you have changed things in any way?
- ✓ How did the fight affect your relationship with this person?
- ✓ How did you feel afterward?
- ✓ Were there any important repercussions?

Write the details of the fight from start to finish, and make it as dramatic as possible. Give meaning to it. And don't forget to include any humor connected with the fight—fights usually are humorous in retrospect. Think about these questions as a way to complete your writing:

Was this incident similar to or different from the way you usually handle conflict?

Did you make any decision about yourself, others, or the world after this fight?

If so, is that decision still affecting your life today?

Fights have built-in climactic interest in them, so use this exercise to create a scene with dramatic structure that builds in intensity and leads to a climax.

Maybe you don't normally remember many of your dreams, but chances are you have had at least one nightmare in your life that you've never forgotten. Nightmares aren't necessarily full of evil people or monsters. They can portray a simple, everyday happening, which for some reason frightens you.

Pick a Nightmare You Vividly Remember

Choose one particular nightmare for this exercise. The nightmare can be a recent one or one from your childhood; it can be a recurring one or one you've had only once.

Close Your Eyes and Let the Sequence of the Dream Unfold

Watch the dream from start to finish as if it were a movie.

Go Back and Run It Through Again, Seeing It Moment by Moment

When you get to the end of the nightmare, go back and let it run through again. This time watch it as if it were a series of still photographs. Notice how you feel as you allow the dream to unfold without any resistance on your part.

Look Closely at All the Characters in the Dream

Focus first on the characters in your dream.

✓ Who are all the people in the dream? Don't leave anyone out.

✓ Where are *you* in the dream?
✓ Who is the central character in the dream other than yourself?
✓ Which character, if any, do you perceive as dangerous to you?
✓ Is anyone part of the dream who doesn't actually appear?

Get a Clear Picture of the Character or Characters Who Seem Dangerous to You

Let this character or characters grow and become even more threatening. Take a good look at your persecutor:

✓ What is the character doing to you or keeping you from doing?
✓ What is the most distinguishing feature of this character?
✓ What is most frightening to you?

Open Your Eyes and Think about the Sequence of the Dream Again

Now, with your eyes open, review the sequence of events in the dream.

✓ Where in your body do you feel the dream?
✓ Was anything or anybody part of the dream but outside the framework of the dream itself? If so, imagine what that missing part or character would be like.
✓ If you could put yourself in the place of the threatening character, how would you feel? What would you do?
✓ Were there any verbal or nonverbal messages given to you through the dream?

There are several ways to write about the nightmare:

Write it out like a simple story, beginning "Once upon a time. . . ."

Write it from the threatening character's point of view.

Draw each visual frame of the dream as if it were a comic strip and then write out a narrative to go with it.

Trace your body experiences both in the dream and after you awoke.

Write about the symbols and what they mean to you; include any "messages" you received.

Think about the dream's meaning and/or intention. What might it be trying to accomplish? Could it be trying to get your attention about something?

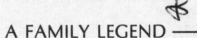

A FAMILY LEGEND

Don't let the word "legend" throw you. A family legend can be any story that has been handed down through the years and has been repeated several times. The story could even be about some family member you've never met. Your task as the recorder of this legend is to take the different oral versions and put them into one unified form. Perhaps your version will one day become the "official" version.

Begin by Thinking Back over the Many Family Stories You've Heard

You might have heard these stories from family members or from others outside your family. Take time to recall as many as you can think of right now.

Select One You Would Like to Put into Writing

✓ Who were the major characters?
✓ When and where did it take place?
✓ What attracts you most about this story?

Recall the First Time You Ever Heard the Story

✓ How old were you?
✓ Where were you?
✓ Who told the story?
✓ Who else was there?

Trace All the Subsequent Times You Heard the Story

Briefly review in your mind, or on paper, all the versions you've heard of this story.

✓ Do they differ significantly?
✓ Who told each of the versions?
✓ What was left out of each version?
✓ What was added?

Decide Which Version You'd Like to Put into Writing

Out of all the versions, pick the one you like the best or the one you think most authentic.

✓ Whose story is this?
✓ What point of view will you use?

Write Down the Story in Any Form You Choose

You can write the story in linear, chronological form—start to finish; or you can turn it into a piece of fiction; or perhaps even put it into ballad form. The choice is yours. If you need an audience, you might choose a younger member of the family and write it for them to read at a later date.

Reflect on the Meaning of this Legend in Your Family

Stories exist within families for a reason. Locate the meaning behind the repetition of this story in your family. Consider these questions:

- ✓ How true is this story? Do facts support it?
- ✓ Why has this story been repeated or handed down?
- ✓ What does the story reveal about my family?
- ✓ How has this story contributed to the dreams, values, and historical experiences of my family?
- ✓ What interests me most about this story?

To take this further and use the story as material for your writing, write it more than once so you can see it from several different points of view. Tell it first through the eyes of the main character and then through the eyes of someone else. Family stories such as these have supplied many writers with material for major works.

The word "puberty" alone is enough to give most of us shivers. Puberty is generally both a time of high excitement and wonder and a time of utter misery and dejection—a seesaw time rarely forgotten.

Stay with the Word "Puberty" for a Few Moments

Ponder the word for a while. Say it over a few times in your mind. What images come to you?

Picture Yourself at the Age of Puberty

Think of yourself at around the age commonly associated with puberty—from 12 to 13.

- ✓ What did you look like?
- ✓ What did you *want* to look like?
- ✓ How did you look in comparison to your friends?

What Was Your Life Like at That Time?

Think about where you lived and with whom.

- ✓ What was going on in your family at the time?
- ✓ How did they respond to you?
- ✓ What were your major thoughts and feelings about yourself?

What Kind of Sexual and/or Romantic Feelings Did You Have?

Awakening sexual feelings usually occur during puberty.

- ✓ Did you have a boyfriend or girlfriend?
- ✓ Were you active sexually?
- ✓ What kind of fantasies were you having?
- ✓ How would you describe your feelings about sex?

Think about the Physical Changes You Underwent

Puberty is a time of great physical change; close your eyes and visualize your body in detail.

- ✓ Go through all the physical problems you were aware of.
- ✓ What were some of your major physical sensations?

How did you feel about your body and its changes?

Locate One Particular Incident That Captures What Puberty Was Like for You

The incident doesn't have to be a big one; just a simple memory that stands as an emblem of puberty for you.

- ✓ Where were you and what were you doing?
- ✓ Who was with you and what part did others play?
- ✓ What happened?
- ✓ What were your most intense feelings about the incident?

Write the incident as much as possible through the eyes of your pubescent self. Pay special attention to the intensity of your feelings and your physical sensations. Who *was* that boy or girl? What happened to him or her?

Sometimes a first love can set the stage for all future loves. Going back to that earliest love and your feelings then might give you some insights into all your other loves throughout the years—and now.

Think Back to the Very First Time You Felt Heart Palpitations for Someone Else

Perhaps your first love was someone in your own family. If so, work with that person if you can't recall your earliest boyfriend or girlfriend. But go back as far in time as possible to an early heartthrob.

Put the Face of Your First Love before Your Inner Eye

Once you select the person, allow the image to grow large, as if on a giant TV screen.

Look Closely at the Physical Details of This Person

Stay with it until you get a clear visual image of your first love.

- ✓ Pinpoint the age of both this person and yourself.
- ✓ Look at all the physical details of the other person—hair, teeth, nose, clothes, and so forth

Recollect a Specific time You Were Together

Now recollect a time you were together and trace the incident as fully as you can. Notice how you acted and how you felt with this person.

Identify Any Other Events Connected with This Early Love

Think about other times, places, and people you associate with your first love.

- ✓ How often were you together?
- ✓ Can you think of other memories?
- ✓ Were other people involved in any way?

Trace the History of This First Love Affair

Follow this love affair from beginning to end. Even if it was just "puppy" love, your feelings were as important to you then as they are today.

- ✓ What attracted you most to your first love?
- ✓ Whatever happened to this person? When was the last time you saw them?
- ✓ How did the relationship progress? Over how many years?
- ✓ How did the relationship finally end?

Write what you learned about romantic relationships from this first love. How was it similar to other romantic relationships you've had since becoming an adult? Do you still have any of those same feelings today?

You might also write this from the point of view of young children. If children "in love" could explain their feelings, what do you think they would say?

Toys have a life of their own—and can become as important as family to children. Doing this exercise several times will help you reclaim some of those special toys you once loved and, in the process, perhaps you'll discover new information about yourself at a particular age.

Make a Random List of Toys You Remember from Your Childhood

Take time to think back over all the toys you used to love and make a list. The list can be either written or mental. Look back over the list and choose the toy that stands out most for you at a particular age, say at age two, age seven, and so on.

Pick One of the Toys You Loved the Most

There are probably several that were your favorites, but choose one of these to work with. Your toy doesn't have to be a typical toy such as a doll or a truck; it can also be a book, a board game, a homemade object, or any item you loved and played with as a child.

Visualize Yourself at the Age When You Owned This Toy

✓ What did you look like?
✓ What were some of the clothes you wore?
✓ Who were some of your playmates?
✓ What were some of the things you did?

Recall Yourself Playing with It

Think of how, when, and where you played with it.

✓ What type of toy was it?
✓ What were all its parts?
✓ What did it look like as a whole?
✓ What could the toy do with your help?
✓ How did you spend most of your time playing with it?

Trace the Toy's History

✓ Who gave it to you? When and where?
✓ How long did you have it?
✓ What were the major events in your toy's life back then?
✓ Where is it now?

Recall the Pleasure of Owning It

Recapture as fully as possible the pleasure you felt in playing with your toy.

✓ What did you like best about it?
✓ What kind of thoughts and feelings did it evoke in you?
✓ What in your later life has given you those same feelings?

In your writing, try to get at what was behind your attachment to this toy. What did it represent to you then, and what does it represent to you now?

You can do this exercise many times, using a snapshot from just about every period of your life to rediscover important feelings you had about yourself and others at that time. Seeing yourself in old snapshots can bring up a lot of buried—sometimes very emotional—memories, so go gently with yourself on this one.

Pick Out an Old Photograph of Yourself from Any Period in Your Life

An informal snapshot is ideal, but if all you have is a formal studio portrait, that's fine. If you can actually hold the photo in your hands, do so. If not, just visualize one you remember. And if memory fails, or you have no photographs, use your imagination to create one.

Study the Photograph Closely

If you have the photograph in hand, you can use a magnifying glass to study the small details. If you don't have an actual photograph, use the one you remember or imagine and mentally project it enlarged onto a screen so that you can look at all the details.

Observe the Setting

- ✓ Is it indoors or outdoors?
- ✓ What season of the year is it?
- ✓ What time of day?
- ✓ What are the specific surroundings within the frame of the photo? What is outside the frame?

Look at Who Else and What Else Is in the Photograph

- ✓ If you're not alone in the photo, who are the other people with you? Take a long slow look at all the others.
- ✓ What else is in the photo, such as animals or inanimate objects?
- ✓ Is anything or anybody missing from this snapshot?
- ✓ Who do you think took the picture?

Examine Yourself in Detail

- ✓ What are you doing in the picture?
- ✓ Look at the expression on your face and what you're wearing.
- ✓ See if you can remember exactly what was going on in your life at this time.
- ✓ Look into your eyes and see if you can remember what you were feeling at the time of the photo.
- ✓ Can you remember wanting something from someone— something you either got or did not?

Recall What Happened Right Before and Right After the Snapshot

- ✓ Where were other members of the family when this shot was taken?
- ✓ What were they doing?
- ✓ Were they conscious of you—what you were doing and feeling?

When you come out of the exercise, begin writing as fast as possible. Don't stop to wonder whether you are being accurate or not. You might think you've made the whole thing up, and that's okay. Chances are, your perceptions are true no matter how fictional they may seem. Photographs, as well as paintings, are excellent story starters.

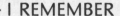 I REMEMBER

Everything that has ever happened to you is still stored in your memory waiting for you to reclaim it. The purpose of this exercise is to take you as far back as you can remember, to your very earliest memory—perhaps even to the moment when you first became aware of being alive.

Set your sights on going back to the preverbal stage of your development, but don't criticize yourself if you can only make it back to grade school or even high school years. As you get your memory flowing, you'll go further back each time you do the exercise.

You will need to do this exercise with your eyes closed, so either taperecord the instructions, which are fairly simple, or read them through a few times.

Get into a Comfortable Position and Close Your Eyes

You can either lie down or sit in a comfortable chair, but take a few moments to become totally relaxed in order to put yourself into a receptive frame of mind.

Visualize Yourself on an Elevator, Descending to an Earlier Age

You are on an elevator at floor 21. The buttons on the elevator number from 18 to B, representing the first 18 years of your life.

- ✓ Push a button and feel yourself descend to that "floor"—an age of your life.
- ✓ When the elevator doors open, step out to the floor and remember yourself at that age.

Retrieve a Memory of Yourself at That Age

Take whatever memory comes to you about that particular age. It can be something as simple as a dress or suit you wore or a remembered snapshot.

Get Back on the Elevator and Push a Lower Button

Get back on the elevator and visualize yourself going down gently and safely. When the doors open, step out into that age and retrieve another memory. Bring it back with you and get on the elevator again.

Push a Button Lower than Six

If possible, go down in the elevator as far as one or two—or even to "B" for basement (or born). Feel yourself descend slowly, floor by floor, into the safe darkness. When the elevator stops, get out and walk around and see what comes to you.

Choose One of These Early Memories to Work With

When you have retrieved a memory that seems important to you, stay with it and keep visualizing it.

- ✓ Where are you?
- ✓ Who's with you?
- ✓ How are you feeling?

✓ What kinds of colors and shapes do you see around you? What sounds and smells?

✓ What are you most aware of?

Stay with the Scene Until You Have Retrieved Buried Details

If you continue to watch the scene with your eyes closed, many other details will come into view.

✓ What is going on around you? What do you notice that you did not notice before?

✓ What can you hear being said by others?

✓ At what point does the scene end?

Return to the Elevator and Come Back Slowly to the Surface, Bringing with You the Memories You Retrieved

Get back on the elevator, allow the doors to close, and push the button marked 21. Feel the elevator rise. Take your time returning. Before opening your eyes, ask yourself these questions: Why is this particular memory important to me? What does it still evoke in me?

Now try to capture in writing the things you saw, heard, and felt. Tell your story as a very young child would see it:

Focus on one short incident—something that happens within minutes

Keep the child's point of view

Use present tense as if it's happening in the moment.

IMAGINATION

Look, I made a hat. . .
Where there never was a hat . . .

—STEPHEN SONDHEIM
"Finishing the Hat"

Imaginings can sometimes take us over and cause us trouble—as in imagining forthcoming disasters, excessive daydreaming, circular conversations in our head, living in fantasies, and so forth. In these cases, the imagination has us. But for *us* to have our imagination and use it as we choose—ah, that can be heaven. Nothing is more important to a writer than a strong and active imagination that can be used as a conscious tool for the craft of writing. See what your imagination brings you from the following exercises:

An Interior Landscape
Becoming an Animal
Another Voice
You Are the Camera
Empty Stage
Sex Change
Erotica
Whisper
The Cheat
Nonsense

Even if you're not an artist, here's your opportunity to "draw" a landscape of your own creation and keep it framed in your imagination—a private place you can return to whenever you like. Read the directions through ahead of time so that you can close your eyes for most of the exercise.

Put Yourself into a Relaxed State of Mind

You can either sit up or lie down for this exercise; just get very comfortable and allow your mind to float. Take a few moments to breathe deeply so that you can be fully relaxed during the process.

Imagine Yourself Walking in a Barren Land

Start by imagining yourself walking through a vast barren land. Nothing is there—no familiar landmarks, no landscape that you recognize. Continue to walk alone for awhile.

As You Continue to Walk, Allow a Landscape to Unfold Around You

In a few moments, you will begin to see a landscape emerge around you as you continue to walk. Pay close attention to all the different images that your imagination creates as you walk.

Stop and Observe Any Unusual Features or Objects That You See

When something seems particularly unusual, stop walking and examine it closely. Get a mental image of it firmly in your mind before continuing your journey.

Take Time to Absorb the Particular Atmosphere of This Landscape

Think about how this landscape differs from others you know.

✓ What is most different about it?
✓ Do you notice any unusual smells and sounds?
✓ What word would you use to describe the atmosphere?

Remove Yourself from the Picture and Look at the Landscape Again

Whenever you feel ready, stop walking and take yourself out of the picture. Now start from the beginning of your walk and, like a camera, slowly survey the entire landscape again from start to finish. Notice whether you change any of the elements as you view it a second time.

Before beginning your writing, jot down a simple drawing just to remind yourself of the shape of the landscape. Then describe your place and explore the personal symbols you have created in your imaginary landscape. This is now a place you can revisit often for relaxation and inspiration—and also perhaps a place you can use as a focus for some of your writing.

Most people have a strong identification with some kind of animal. If you do, here's a chance to find out what's behind your connection with a particular animal. If you don't, work with whatever kind of animal pops into your head.

Become Aware of Your Body

Stretch out your body and relax all of your muscles by first tensing each of them and then letting them go. Start with your toes and travel slowly up your body, contracting and releasing each part. Keeping your eyes closed as you do this will intensify your sensory awareness of all the parts of your body.

Visualize an Animal in Front of You

If you haven't already thought of an animal, take the first animal that comes into your head. Stay with your visualization long enough to see a particular animal rather than a conventional picture of one. You might even come up with an imaginary one.

Look the Animal Over from Head to Foot

First walk around the animal and look closely at its features.

- ✓ How is it shaped?
- ✓ What unusual characteristics does it have?
- ✓ What kind of body covering?
- ✓ What kind of teeth, eyes, hair?

Consider This Animal's Nature

What is the basic nature of this animal?

- ✓ What is its temperament?
- ✓ How does it get along in the world?
- ✓ How does this animal respond to other animals?
- ✓ How does it respond to human beings?

Observe How It Moves

Spend some time observing how this particular animal moves its body. Is there anything unusual about the way it moves?

Become Aware of Your Own Basic Animal Nature

Become conscious of your breathing as an involuntary act—like that of an animal. Think of the "animal" aspects of yourself.

Imagine That You Have Become Your Animal

When you feel ready, allow yourself to become your animal. Get into its body and observe the world through its eyes.

- ✓ What does it see?
- ✓ How does it view the world?

Write down your observations, either from your own point of view or allowing the animal to speak. Think of your connection to this particular animal.

Does it have any thoughts, ideas, or secrets to tell you?
How might you use some of the animal's qualities in your own life?
What could it teach you about how to move your body?

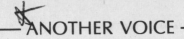

This is an exercise in the power of suggestion—an imagination strengthener and a way to create characters in your writing. Leaf through some magazines and cut out half a dozen photographs of real people (as opposed to models in ads). Pick the ones who attract your eye, who seem to call out to you.

Choose the Character Who Interests You the Most

Spend some time choosing the person you want to work with.

- ✓ What makes this person interesting?
- ✓ What quality most attracts you?

Put the Picture Before You and Imagine the Life of This Person

Look closely at the photograph. Take as much time as you need in order to experience the person as a real human being—someone you might know.

- ✓ Where does the person live? What country, town, type of dwelling?
- ✓ What do they do for a living?
- ✓ What is their sex life like?
- ✓ Who are the members of their family? What other relationships do they have?

Imagine This Person's Character Traits

Make your character as specific as possible.

✓ What are their particular quirks?
✓ What kind of temperament do they have?
✓ What words would you use to describe this person to someone?

See the Person in Action

Visualize your character in some activity.

✓ How do they move?
✓ What do they look like when they are walking, running, and so forth.
✓ How do they talk?
✓ How do they act when other people are around?

Give This Person A Voice

Let the character speak, and allow this "other voice" to say whatever it wants to. Record this person's story.

Once you've recorded this character's story, you can either develop the character's life further or choose another picture from your group. Keep all the pictures in an envelope so that you can call on them next time you want to do the exercise. You can also put two or three of them before you and see what scene develops among them.

Another way to use the exercise is to ask this character for advice. Let the character speak, and enjoy the process of letting another person take over your problem. Later you can decide whether to accept or reject the advice.

YOU ARE THE CAMERA

In this exercise, you are the camera, recording the scene that takes place before you. You're going to first dress the set with scenery, people, and objects and then watch and record the scene that develops. Read through the whole exercise first to get ready because you'll be working with your eyes closed as much as possible.

Study This List or Have It Read to You

You can memorize this list or have someone read it to you—or read it into a tape recorder:

A green bottle
An oak table
A woman in white
Two men
A lawnmower
Sunlight

Close Your Eyes and Pretend That You Are a Camera

Feel the darkness around you as if you are the inside of a camera. As a camera, you will objectively observe and record what you see.

Visualize the Items One at a Time

Give yourself space between items so that each one can "arrange" itself where it wants to be. After you've placed the items, including characters, into relationship with one another, pan the entire scene as a movie camera does.

Allow the People and Objects to Come to Life

Let the scene come to life any way it chooses.

Watch the Scene Unfold, and Mentally Record What You See and Hear

Allow the scene to unfold fully. Don't rush it—relax and let the action go on as long as it likes or until you feel you have taken everything in that you want to. The characters and objects may surprise you.

See If One of the Characters Dominates the Scene

If a character wants to take over the scene, let it do so. This is a good way to discover strong characters who can lead you to an unusual story.

Open Your Eyes and Replay the Scene in Your Imagination

When you're ready, let the scene dissolve. Open your eyes, but before you begin to write, replay the scene in your imagination. You may find yourself adding details and ideas and developing the action further.

Write Down the Story These Characters Want to Tell

If you've allowed one of the characters to take over the story, you can record what it has to say and then go back and let the story take a different turn—change the events or let other characters take over.

Use this exercise often to discover new characters or story ideas. You can make up your own random lists as you go along, or you can use the three lists below. Feel free to add or subtract any item.

An apple	An elderly couple	A pair of sneakers
Rain	A forest	The ocean
A child	A radio	A car
A hat	A piece of paper	Two teenagers
Three adults	Strong wind	Heat
A clothespin	An animal	A clock

———————— EMPTY STAGE ————————

The title itself gives you some idea of what you'll be doing in this exercise: peopling an empty stage with actors, scenery, and props and then setting them into action. This gives you another approach to creating dramatic scenes out of your own head.

If you can actually put yourself in front of an empty stage—a school auditorium or a small playhouse—that's fine. Most likely you will be creating everything, including the empty stage, with your imagination—and that's just as good.

Close Your Eyes Briefly and Imagine an Empty Stage

You've no doubt seen many different stages in your life. Just visualize any kind of stage you can remember.

Imagine Yourself Seated in the Audience, Watching the Stage

In your imagination, put yourself into the audience in front of an empty stage. At this point, you can either keep your eyes closed or open them if you can still keep the image of the stage in front of you.

Place a Few Props around the Stage

Slowly begin to set a scene by imagining a few props. Keep the furnishings and props as simple as possible, but choose objects that can be used in an interesting way.

Light the Stage

Watch the lights on the stage come up. Take enough time to get exactly the quality of light you want on the stage. Vary the tints and shadings until you have created precisely the atmosphere you want.

Bring Some Characters onto the Stage

You can people the stage with as few or as many characters as you like. Even one character will do. You might also start with a few characters and add others as you go along.

Start the Action in the Middle of the Play

Begin the action and watch it unfold. This is not the beginning of the play. Other scenes and action have taken place before this moment.

- ✓ What has happened prior to this?
- ✓ What is going on right at this moment?

Let the Characters Speak

Listen to the dialogue (or monologue) that is going on. Stay with this awhile until you hear real people talking.

✓ What is each of the characters saying?
✓ To whom is each character speaking?

Observe Each of the Characters in Detail

Use your imagination to develop each of the characters into real human beings.

✓ What do each of them look like?
✓ What is each doing?
✓ What are some of their unusual mannerisms?
✓ What do each of them want? What is at stake?

Turn off the Lights

End the scene by darkening the stage.

✓ What was the main effect of this scene?
✓ What idea, image, or atmosphere lingers after the scene is over?

Before you begin writing, imagine the next scene. Then start writing down your scene, keeping in mind what you know will happen next but concentrating solely on showing your scene in action. Don't tell it indirectly; put yourself and the reader right into the middle of it, just as a scene in a play does. It doesn't have to make absolute sense. You are working primarily to achieve dramatic structure, dialogue, and character development.

Here's your chance to get a feeling of what you might be like had you been born the opposite sex. Get comfortable for this one by stretching out on the floor, bed, or sofa.

Visualize Yourself from Head to Foot the Way You Are Now

Become very aware of your body and its sensations. Slowly visualize yourself from head to foot exactly as you are right now. Don't move your imagination from a body part until you've gotten a vivid picture of it in your mind.

Imagine Yourself Waking Up in Bed on a Sunny Morning

You awake and start to stretch. Everything seems to be the same—same bed, same bedroom. You think for a moment about what you did the night before.

You Slowly Realize That Something about You Is Different

You can tell, even before you open your eyes, that something is different. In fact something is *very* different. You lie there with your eyes closed, still half asleep, trying to get the sense of what is going on. Gradually you begin to realize that something about your body has changed.

You Discover That You Have Had a Sex Change

You run your hands over your body and a shock ripples through you. You can't take it in all at once. You open your eyes and look at yourself: Somehow or other during the night, your sex has changed.

You Go to the Mirror and Look at Your New Body

You look with amazement at your body in the mirror. You're still the same person. Nothing has changed about you emotionally or mentally. But physically you have become a member of the opposite sex. Take in all the physical changes that have occurred in your body.

Let the Story Unfold However You Like

Once you've gotten a clear sense of the new you, let the story go in any direction you like.

- ✓ What happens next?
- ✓ Who else is in the house with you?
- ✓ How do you handle this change?
- ✓ Where do you go from here? What do you do?
- ✓ How do other people react to you?

Since this is a fantasy, you might find yourself writing a short piece of fiction that just takes off in the direction it wants to go. But if you write about how you were affected by imagining yourself as another sex, explore in detail how this would change you.

How would you feel about it?
Would it change the way you do things? The way you view the world?
What kind of person would you be?
What present knowledge would you take with you?

Even if you're not too interested in writing erotica, there's something to be gained from doing so—and more than just titillating fantasies. Erotic writing can be an excellent way to put more power into your writing. Because sexual experiences are usually moments of intense physical and emotional expression, you start out ahead by having something substantial to describe.

Think Objectively of a Sexual Scene

You can use something personal—your own experience or fantasy—or use an idea from a book or movie. The point is to stand back as an objective observer.

Create the Characters You Need to Express the Erotic Scene

You can start with one or two characters and add others if you like. Take time to get a strong mental image of what they look and act like.

- ✓ Describe each of them physically, head to toe. What are some of their distinguishing characteristics?
- ✓ Give each of them some unusual mental or emotional characteristic—make them individuals. Avoid cliché representations such as the sex kitten, the over-sized stud. Make them *human,* with both physical and psychological flaws.

Put Them into Action

Now just sit back, observe, and enjoy.

- √ Where is this taking place?
- √ What are they doing? Be specific in noting each action as it unfolds.
- √ Do you observe anything unusual about them or their actions?

Add an Unusual Ingredient

Once you've got the scene going as erotically as possible, introduce some unusual turn: an unannounced character, an unexpected event, some funny or offbeat action.

Check in with Yourself

Take note of your memories and feelings as you watch the scene. Use the reality of your experiences and feelings to add more truth to it.

Stay with the Scene a Little Longer

Give the scene a bit more time to unfold; it may take a turn that will surprise and delight you. When you're ready, close shop.

Now comes the writing. You may have to just sketch in the scene at first and then go back and fill in details, but give yourself enough time to describe everything you saw, felt, and heard. Write past any resistances you might have about whether your writing is silly, disgusting, or trite. When you find yourself lapsing into centerfold or movie clichés, close your eyes and get more specific details from your scene.

Listening in on other people's conversations, especially if they sound full of emotion and meaning, is usually irresistible. No matter what's being said, we find ourselves filling in the blanks and coming up with our own scenario for what's going on. This exercise asks you to imagine listening in on a conversation between two people (you can also go to a public place and actually do so) and then write down what you hear.

Imagine Yourself in a Public Setting

Close your eyes for a few moments and imagine yourself in a public setting—a restaurant, a park, an elevator, a bus. Take time to create the details of the place.

Imagine You Hear Two People Nearby Whispering to Each Other

You see two strangers nearby engaged in an intense private conversation. They don't know that you are observing them because they are too absorbed in their conversation.

Take a Look at Each of the People

Notice what each of the people looks like.

- ✓ What do you surmise about them and their relationship?
- ✓ What do you imagine their lives are like?
- ✓ What is the current situation that has led to the conversation?
- ✓ What are they doing as they talk?

Listen to Their Conversation

Now listen in on what they are saying as they whisper to each other. Remember: This is a private conversation and you are eavesdropping. They are completely unaware of you.

- ✓ Record the dialogue between them as accurately as possible. Give yourself enough time and space for the conversation to unfold completely.
- ✓ Try to capture the cadence, accent, and unusual expressions of each person's speech.

Make Up a Story about Them

As you listen to them whisper, what is the story that goes on in your head about these two people? What can you tell about them after you have heard them talking?

Begin your writing by objectively reporting the conversation exactly as you overheard it. Then you can go further and make up a story about these two people based on your observations and what you heard. Perhaps you can develop your piece into a short vignette or a story—or even a novel.

———————— THE CHEAT ————————

Sometimes a simple character tag can put a full-blown picture of a person in your head. In this exercise, you're going to create a character called "The Cheat" from the ground up, relying solely on your imagination. Then you can use the exercise to create other character types.

Close Your Eyes and Repeat "The Cheat" Over to Yourself Several Times

Keep recreating the words until you begin to get images, other words, or ideas.

- √ What images come into your mind?
- √ What word associations?

Visualize a Character Who Fits the Name The Cheat

Start to create a character in your imagination that you think of as The Cheat. Go for the off-beat.

- √ Is this person male or female?
- √ How old are they?
- √ Where do they live?
- √ What's their name?

Look at the Character's Physical Appearance

Take the time to create a full physical picture.

- √ How tall are they?
- √ What's the color of their hair and eyes?
- √ What is their body like?
- √ Do they have any deformities or unusual features?
- √ What kind of clothes do they wear?

Look at the Character's Mannerisms

- √ Do they have any noticeable or unusual body gestures that they use regularly?
- √ How do they sound when they talk?
- √ How do they look when they walk?

Speculate on the Character's Background

Give this person a real history.

- ✓ What kind of childhood did they have?
- ✓ What kind of sex life?
- ✓ Do they have a spouse or lover?
- ✓ What is the biggest secret that they keep from others?

Imagine the Character's Habits of Thought and Action

- ✓ What do they consistently think about?
- ✓ What do they consistently do?
- ✓ Are there any surprises in their thoughts or actions?

Put The Cheat into Action

Close your eyes and see The Cheat in action. Create a situation in which The Cheat is the central character and affects other people.

- ✓ What has taken place prior to this?
- ✓ What will happen after this scene?
- ✓ Who wants what?
- ✓ Who gets what?

Visualize a Close-Up of The Cheat in a Surprising Action

Let the scene develop and see if you can create some surprising action for The Cheat to take—perhaps something out of character.

How Do Others Respond to The Cheat?

- ✓ What is the major feeling The Cheat inspires in others?
- ✓ What are The Cheat's relationships usually like?

Speculate on What Motivates The Cheat

Think about how The Cheat feels and thinks.

- ✓ What is the cheat trying to accomplish?
- ✓ What does The Cheat really want?
- ✓ In what ways is The Cheat inconsistent?

After you have gathered more information than you think you need, write a character sketch of The Cheat. Make every effort to raise the sketch above the trite and expected so the character becomes a fully rounded human being.

Adapt this exercise to take other traditional stereotypes and give them new dimensions. Make up your own or try some of the following:

The Hunk	The Criminal	The Hustler
The Gambler	The Old Maid	The Manipulator
The Sex Kitten	The Innocent	The Rock Star

——————— NONSENSE ———————

This last exercise is a departure of sorts—an invitation for you to go "off the wall," give up control, and allow some kind of strange voice to take over. There's always a background voice going on in our heads. Here's a chance to tune into one of them and allow your imagination to have full play. Your job is to relax, listen, and then record what you hear, as if you are taking dictation.

Put Yourself into a State of Reverie

Create a state of reverie by lounging in a chair or on a sofa. Make yourself as relaxed as possible.

Half-Close Your Eyes

You need to keep your eyes open so that you can write fast, but lower them to a semi-closed position so that your vision is focused entirely downward.

Listen for a Voice in Your Head

Tune into your inner world. Don't write a word until you actually hear someone else's voice speaking in your ear. It's important not to begin writing until you feel "visited" by this other voice. If you stay quiet and receptive, you will soon hear one. Don't give up.

Write Down Rapidly What You Hear the Voice Saying

The moment you hear the voice, start writing fast and without any thought whatsoever. Don't think or judge. Just follow what the voice says step by step and try to keep up with it. No matter what the voice says, write it down without comment. Even if what you're writing is surreal or senseless, stay with it.

When the Voice Stops, Make a Switch

When you come to what feels like an ending—when the voice stops or you feel you can't stay with it anymore—make a conscious switch of some kind. You can do this by allowing another voice to speak. You can also do it by recalling the first voice and making a switch in pronouns; for example, if the first voice used "I," now begin a piece using "you."

You might be surprised at what you've written. Perhaps you'll think all you got is a lot of garbage, but don't be too quick to judge. Maybe you've taken down a nice phrase or even invented some new words that could be important to you later.

If you're pleased with the outcome of the exercise, repeat it many times to develop your imagination in a new way. These voices might be different parts of you—or real characters—clamoring to come to life through your writing.

Going On

This is the last chapter and it's about going on—*you* going on. I'll still be smuggled into these pages waiting for the next reader. But you will go on from here and wave to me from your mountaintop. Come back to visit, sure. But don't hang around in here too long or too often. Dip in, take what you want, then run to your quill and parchment and write that book you were thinking about even before you opened this one.

So what is the point of this chapter? The point is to give you some ideas and inspiration for going further with your writing. Maybe you're already doing that; but just in case you aren't, I want to leave you with more than a notebook of fragmentary exercises.

You can start with repetition of the exercises. In the appendix you'll see an alphabetical listing of the exercises with page numbers so you can easily locate the ones you want to do again. You'll find great value in doing the same exercise several times. You'll get new material or get at the same material from different angles—both good ways to build longer narratives around one theme.

Also in the appendix are two alternate groupings for the exercises. The first grouping is based on subject categories such as Childhood, Self-Awareness, and so forth. The second grouping is based on writerly concerns in case you want to work on specific writing techniques, such as story ideas, character development, voice. Again, these are arbitrary groupings, and many of the exercises overlap from one group to the next.

I also want to leave you with some suggestions for turning the exercises into longer pieces of writing, as well as suggestions for having more fun with them.

To turn the exercises into longer pieces you can

Take one particular theme you see showing up in your exercises and go further with that idea.

Choose a general topic and pick an exercise from each category to develop different aspects of the topic.

Take one of the characters or situations and develop it into a complete story.

Take one experience and write it several times to develop it in different ways.

To have more fun with the exercises, you can

Randomly choose a title from one group and a title from another and use them together creatively. For example, you could take "A Nightmare" and couple it with "An Eating Experience" or "Another Voice" and put it together with "Scars."

Take different characters from different exercises, put them together, and cook up a plot for them—for example, put "Your Favorite Enemy," "The Cheat," and one of the characters from "You Are the Camera" together and see what happens.

Since many of these exercises delve into self-analysis, you can put a number of them together and do a "mood" autobiography of yourself.

Put the title of each exercise on a separate slip of paper, put each slip into a separate envelope, seal the envelopes, and then choose one on a prearranged schedule. This is a good way to force yourself to experiment with all the exercises—even the ones you resist.

Interchange parts of different exercises. Do the first three steps of one exercise and the last steps of another exercise and try to make meaning out of it—for example, do steps 1 to 3 of "Repeat Performance" and then switch to steps 4 to 7 of "The Biggest Fight." Having to put unrelated events together keeps your mind flexible and forces your imagination into service.

Make up your own exercises. At this point, you should have many good ideas of your own.

So now I'm going to bow out of here with two barking orders.

First, *read*. It's that simple. Reading is more important to your writing than anything else I can think of. And don't read too many how-to books. Read the great writers, the great thinkers. A special way to read as a writer is to read with a purpose before going to sleep at night. Choose particular writers who can teach you what you want to learn—say Woody Allen for wild humor and outlandish actions; Grace Paley for voice and character; Loren Eiseley for turning on your sense of wonder; Delmore Schwartz for using dreams as story material; Gurdjieff for shaking up your ideas about reality; William Faulkner for hypnotic prose; Colette for voluptuousness; Eudora Welty for place; Ray Bradbury for making the real seem fantastic and vice versa; some of the best poets— Rilke, Lorca, Millet—for planting magnificent sentences in your head. Don't read only to put yourself to sleep. Ease into a state of relaxed attention and then read with the purpose of reseeding your own mental garden while you sleep.

After this chapter, you'll find a short list of books that have been valuable to me in my writing and thinking. I didn't include literary works because I take it for granted that you have your own favorites and are reading some of them regularly. The list includes a few books I think are important to writers and a few I've found important for living. This was the toughest part of the book for me to write because there were hundreds of books to choose from which have become intertwined with my life. But I always like a book that ends with a list of other books, so that's exactly what you'll find at the end of this one.

And the last word before I say goodbye is this: *Always cut what you write down to a manageable size.* Write long, long novels, books, plays, narrative poems—of course. But think about them in small slices. Rather than fighting with huge ideas, fall in love with little pieces of writing, one piece at a time: a description, a paragraph, one scene, one character. Just throw your perfect self out the penthouse window and write a little of this and a little of that—things you've been waiting to write. Then watch those pieces pile up into something that will eventually make even you smile. Bit by bit. Bean by bean. Yes indeed. That *is* the way everything gets done.

SPECIAL BOOKS

A Few Books on Writing

Appelbaum, Judith. *How to Get Happily Published*. New York: Harper & Row, 1988; NAL/Plume, 1989.

Bradbury, Ray. *Zen in the Art of Writing*. Santa Barbara: CAPRA Press, 1990.

Brande, Dorothea. *Becoming a Writer*. Los Angeles: J. P. Tarcher, 1981. (Orig. pub., Harcourt Brace, 1934.)

Dillard, Annie. *The Writing Life*. New York: Harper & Row, 1989.

Elbow, Peter. *Writing without Teachers*. New York: Oxford University Press, 1973.

Garrison, Roger. *How a Writer Works*. New York: Harper & Row, 1981.

Goldberg, Natalie. *Writing Down the Bones*. Boston: Shambhala Publications, 1986.

Ueland, Brenda. *If You Want to Write*. St. Paul: Graywolf Press, 1987. (Orig. pub., G. P. Putnam's Sons, 1938.)

A Few Books on Living

Almaas, A. H. *Essence*. York Beach, ME: Samuel Weiser, 1986.

Bérthèrat, Therese, and Carol Bernstein. *The Body Has Its Reasons*. New York: Random House, 1977; Avon, 1977.

Bosnak, Robert. *A Little Course in Dreams*. Boston: Shambhala, 1988.

Brooks, Charles. *Sensory Awareness*. New York: Felix Morrow, 1986.

Cary, Joyce. *Art and Reality*. New York: Harper & Brothers, 1958.

Eiseley, Loren. *The Unexpected Universe*. New York: Harcourt Brace, 1969.

Field, Joanna. *A Life of One's Own*. Los Angeles: J. P. Tarcher, 1981. (Orig. pub., Chatto and Windus, 1936.)

Gendlin, Eugene. *Focusing*. New York: Bantam, 1982.

Houston, Jean. *The Possible Human*. Los Angeles: J. P. Tarcher, 1982.

Laing, R. D. *The Divided Self*. New York: Pantheon, 1962; Penguin, 1971.

Lowen, Alexander. *Fear of Life*. New York: Macmillan, 1980.

Lockhart, Russell. *Words as Eggs*. Dallas: Spring Publications, 1983.

Mindell, Arnold. *Working with the Dreaming Body*. London: Routledge and Kegan Paul, 1985.

Needleman, Jacob. *The Heart of Philosophy*. New York: Alfred A. Knopf, 1982; Bantam, 1982.

Acknowledgments

I'm deeply grateful for all the silent contributors to this book, especially to:

Nassau Community College, Garden City, New York, for giving me the classes in which to develop these exercises and for a sabbatical—time and financial support—to complete the book.

The Open Center in New York City which gave me the opportunity to test the exercises with adult and professional writers. Thanks to Adele Heyman and Ralph White who got me started.

The Esalen Institute, Big Sur, California, where so much of my writing has flourished. I'm especially grateful to Bette Dingman and the Work Study Program.

All my students through the years—who've always managed to turn the tables and become my teachers. Special thanks to my students at Nassau Community College and to Tine Byrsted, Iva Fischman, and Emilie Borg, who continued informal classes with me and helped me refine some of the exercises.

Friends and teaching colleagues: Kathryn Feldman, Virginia Kirk, Polly Marshall, Nell Ann Pickett, Aishah Rahman, and especially Jay Silverman and Diana Wienbroer, for encouragement and help in countless ways.

Judith Appelbaum and Berenice Hoffman for both personal and professional assistance; Susan Randol, my editor at HarperCollins, who gave me freedom mixed with solid editorial support; Helene Berinsky for her beautiful and functional design, and to Stefanie Woodbridge whose priceless contributions are on every page of this book.

Members of my writing group, those dauntless souls—Anne Bianchi, Russell Dian, Susan Etkind, Jim Fahey, John Garafolo, Trader Selkirk—who never let me get away with anything and gave me wise critiques in the book's earliest beginnings.

Those who gave me ideas for some of the exercises: I'm indebted to Roger Garrison for "A Moment of Delight," Ralph Nazareth for "Sex Change," Trader Selkirk for "Becoming an Animal," Arnold Bennet for "A Throw-It-in-the-Fire Confession from *Self and Self-Management*" (New York: George Doran, 1918), and to Dorothea Brande for "A 5-Minute Concentration Exercise" from *Wake Up and Live* (New York: Simon and Schuster, 1936).

R. D. Laing for teaching me that a book deadline is actually a lifeline and that the end of one book can become the beginning for another.

Bill Russo for leading me into so many productive places; Marty Bigelow Singletary who sat with me, body and soul, as I began this book; Russell Bosworth, Michael Lambert, George Lichter, and Pearl Melniker for extra measures of support through the years.

James Archie Hughes III and David Farris Hughes, my sons, and two of my most cherished friends; my sister and brother, Gloria Abraham and Joseph Farris, for decades of loving attention.

Many other friends and family members, too numerous to name, who have encouraged my writing and cheerfully moved aside for it without abandoning me.

And, ah yes, to the cafés on the upper West Side of New York City—Au Petit Beurre, Cafe Lalo, The Hungarian Pastry Shop, and Bob Nasr's Golden Eagle Restaurant—warm, noisy havens for stir-crazy writers.

Elaine Hughes
New York City
April 1990

Index

SUBJECT CATEGORIES

Memorable Moments

People and Places

Nature

Observations

Other Realms

WRITING TECHNIQUE CATEGORIES

Story Ideas

Scenes and Situations

Creating Characters

Description

Voice and Dialogue

Discovering and Adding Meaning

ALPHABETICAL LIST OF EXERCISES